Praise

'It reads like a rich mentoring conversation, personal, honest and deeply reflective, blending the human and business sides of leadership in a powerful way.'

— **Anette de Bruin**, organisational development expert

'The book is filled with pearls of wisdom, not only on leadership but on how to live a full and fulfilled life. Simple to read, yet rich in depth and insight.'

— **Dr Guido Bartalena**, general manager

'Reading this book lowered my blood pressure. Håkan illuminates the way out of the trap between short-term results and long-term resilience. Fresh, hopeful and highly relevant.'

— **Josh Jordan**, senior healthcare leader

HÅKAN JOHANSSON

THE CARE FACTOR

Leading with Care for Self, People, Results and Values

Rethink

First published in Great Britain in 2026
by Rethink Press (www.rethinkpress.com)

The stories and examples throughout *The Care Factor* come from real experiences. While some details have been adjusted to protect the privacy of individuals and organisations, the essence of each story remains true, and the emotions, dilemmas and decisions described are authentic.

Ant by Palukx from Noun Project

Contents

Foreword

Leaders are entrusted with responsibility – for a business, a team and the people whose work touches customers, stakeholders and society. Their legitimacy stems from impact: are the team, the customers and the organisation better off because of their leadership? True leadership must make a positive difference.

In today's complex and volatile world, this is demanding work. Making a difference means balancing competing goals: managing today's business while preparing for tomorrow, driving performance while enabling growth, thrilling customers while protecting the bottom line. Management builds systems and efficiency; leadership orchestrates transformation – of people, business models and the organisation as a whole. Leaders ask others to step into the unknown, to leave what feels comfortable and to embrace uncertainty. No one can provide certainty; each leader must navigate ambiguity responsibly.

How well you do this is not determined by knowledge alone. The deeper question is: How much do you care?

Do you care enough about the business to go deep in your understanding, face performance gaps, pursue opportunities that demand extra effort and make the hard trade-offs? Do you have the courage to do what is necessary to set the business up for lasting success? The answers to those questions determine how the business can grow and thrive.

Do you care enough about people to engage in real dialogue, to listen deeply and to offer honest feedback – both positive and constructive? Will you take time to understand potential, open doors and stand behind people when they are challenged, while also coaching and stretching them? The answers to those questions determine whether people will open up to you – and truly engage.

Håkan writes about the substance of leadership – what lies beyond knowledge, ideology and the overly simplistic 'just do this' formulas. His work goes to the heart of the matter: Do you care enough – about people, the business, society and yourself – to be trustworthy, and is that trust justified by your actions?

Care cannot be faked. People have sharp antennae for leaders who are self-serving or out of their depth. They see whether you care by watching what you do when no one else is looking. Regardless of skill, the level of care you show shapes trust, engagement and credibility – and with it, your impact and natural authority.

Care begins with self-care. In today's fast-paced environment, many leaders neglect it. They are too busy to recover, pause and think. Under chronic cognitive and emotional overload, attention narrows, self-awareness fades and perspective collapses. You miss signals, understand less and default to short-term problem-solving. The busyness habit exacts a high price – from the leader, the team and the organisation. Sustainable self-care means balancing intensity with recovery: deliberately creating space to replenish energy and regain perspective so you can take in reality, understand people and think strategically.

Self-care is often hardest for caring leaders. It is no coincidence that Håkan himself had to experience a health crash that opened his eyes to its importance. Some leaders assume responsibility too early and continue to carry burdens that aren't theirs to hold; others become addicted to the adrenaline of constant activity. If you find yourself sprinting without pause, reflect on the difference between firefighting and leading. Adopting sustainable self-care routines – and anchoring them in your calendar – is not a nice-to-have but a must-have for enduring leadership. Setting healthy boundaries is part of that discipline: clarifying roles, upholding standards and protecting time for renewal.

Caring for people is a prerequisite for trust and influence. My school-age children already know which teacher truly cares and which one merely 'does the job'. People embrace feedback and stretch themselves when they feel cared for; they resist when they feel managed from a distance. Research calls genuine care for people individual consideration – a core dimension of transformational leadership and a strong predictor of engagement and performance. People want to be seen, heard and appreciated, but caring for people is not the same as caretaking. Fear-driven leaders over-protect, solve problems for others and quietly remove ownership. Caring leaders listen and give space – but they also challenge. They tell the truth, even when it's hard, because withholding honest feedback is unethical: it robs people of the chance to grow. Caring leaders show empathy and hold people accountable to become more than they currently are – because they see potential and they care enough to demand growth.

Caring for the business is a prerequisite for sustainable performance. Today's results are the outcome of yesterday's decisions. Business is the great game of innovation; to stay relevant, organisations must perform today and continuously reinvent themselves while staying true to their purpose. In times of success, it's easy to ride the wave, milk the cow and defer change to a successor. Leaders who truly care think from the future – they take responsibility for both today and tomorrow. They make timely, sometimes painful, decisions: for example, exiting a legacy product to fund a new platform rather than milking the old until decline is irreversible.

Caring for society widens the lens. A CEO I once worked with noted that continually raising performance expectations is essential for business success but can conflict with society's need to provide meaningful work for more than the top percentile. He recognised his organisation's responsibility towards society – especially in times of strength. Care at this level means building inclusive pipelines, creating mid-career upskilling paths, or partnering with schools and communities so that performance and contribution rise together.

Caring leaders think holistically. These dimensions of care are interdependent, and caring leaders manage those links deliberately. Caring for business and people simultaneously means thinking deeply about what must be achieved and who should lead each part – then entrusting the right challenge to the right person and offering support and coaching. Thinking from the future naturally raises the question of succession, which leads to developing talent. Caring holistically allows leaders to act like great coaches: close to each player – caring, challenging and coaching – yet decisive about who plays which game so the team can win.

There is, however, a price to caring. The more you care, the more you invest – and the more vulnerable you become. When people you care about leave, it hurts. When a bet for the business fails, it hurts. Many leaders learn to distance themselves so they don't get hurt; they use detachment as armour. Yet caring requires vulnerability – the willingness to go all in and trust your ability to absorb pain and setbacks. Only then will others truly open up to you. This does not contradict setting healthy practical boundaries.

Håkan is not your typical author. He is a leader with decades of practical experience who has walked the path he describes. I have worked with Håkan for many years and have witnessed his leadership impact grow over time. First, he found his 'true north'. Then he opened himself to others' needs and developed a distinct caring leadership style – balancing deep care for people with profound care for the business. Later, he broadened his perspective to include society, inviting his team to reflect on the organisation's role in a wider context. He leads with care in every fibre – that is why people who once worked with him still reach out for guidance years later.

I hope you care enough to read this book to the end. It is truly worth it. Inside, you will find a practical path to becoming the caring leader your deeper self, your team, your customers and society deserve.

Dr Joachim Stempfle, Founder of atrain

Introduction: The Care Factor In Leadership

Every leader I have met carries both strengths and blind spots. We all want to grow, yet we often struggle to know where to begin.

In today's world of accelerating change, complexity and uncertainty, one truth has become clear to me: to navigate what lies ahead, we must not become harder. We must become more human. We must learn to lead with care.

This is a book about how care – for self, people, results and values – can become the defining factor of leadership in the twenty-first century.

I have written this book for leaders at every scale – from those running small teams or businesses to those leading complex global organisations – because while contexts differ, the essence of leadership is always human. The Care Factor applies wherever people depend on you, whether you lead two people or twenty thousand.

A moment for care

Like many leaders, I have been shaped by moments that demanded difficult choices – times when values, people and business realities collided. One such moment arrived suddenly, and for many of us, it marked the beginning of a new reality.

Do you remember where you were, or what you did, on the morning of 24 February 2022 – the day the news broke that Russia had crossed the border into Ukraine and the threat of invasion became a brutal reality?

I do. I will never forget what happened in the days that followed – not for what it revealed about geopolitics, but for what it revealed about people, and about leadership.

It was one of those moments that shifted from distant headlines to daily life. What had been something we watched on screens was suddenly sitting in my office, shaping decisions we had to make in real time. The war wasn't an abstract event anymore – it was in our meetings, in our hearts and in the faces of the people I worked with.

At the time, our customer support for Russia was handled out of Poland, where many of our Russian-speaking agents were Ukrainian. When the war began, some of them told us they could no longer take calls from Russian customers.

It was a true dilemma. On one hand, this was their job. We could have insisted: 'This is your role. If you won't do it, perhaps you don't belong here.'

On the other hand, how could we ask Ukrainian colleagues – whose families were under threat, whose friends were fighting for survival – to serve Russian customers as if nothing had happened?

We had to choose: Enforce the rule, ignore the reality or find another way?

We chose compassion and common sense. We listened. We gave space.

In the short term, we shifted responsibilities. Over time, we transitioned the Russian support back into Russia. Here is the remarkable part: the very same Ukrainian agents helped us hand over the process. They supported the transition not because they were forced to but because they felt seen, respected and cared for.

That moment taught me something I will never forget: leadership is not only about processes, efficiency or numbers. It is about care. Care for people in their humanity. Care for results that organisations depend on. Care for the values we choose to uphold when it matters most.

About this book

This book is about the care factor in leadership. It is not a trend or a quick fix; it was born from questions I have asked myself again and again:

- What truly lasts in leadership?
- What principles are universal, regardless of time, culture or industry?
- What makes some leaders build trust and resilience while others crumble when the context shifts?

The Care Factor is my attempt to answer these questions. It is a manifesto for a new kind of leadership – one that balances performance with humanity, vision with humility, and ambition with responsibility.

These pages are written not as universal truths but as lived experiences and invitations for reflection. I believe that leadership is best understood not through theory alone but through the moments that test our values, shape our character and remind us what truly matters.

Throughout this journey, you will meet stories, paradoxes and reflections that bring care to life in practical ways. You will be challenged to pause, reflect and take small but meaningful steps forward – not towards perfection but towards progress. The stories and examples come from real experiences – moments I have lived, led through and learnt from. They reflect the people and situations that have shaped my understanding of leadership over many years. These reflections are written from the perspective of today – shaped by time, distance and a deeper understanding of what care in leadership truly means. There are moments I wish I could relive, to apply the insights I now hold more clearly. That is, perhaps, the essence of leadership itself: learning forward, one experience at a time.

You'll also meet a small but persistent voice – Li'l Anti – who questions everything I say about care. Anti isn't just a sceptic; he's also trying, in his own way, to change himself and others. His story unfolds through short interludes – fables that give you a chance to pause, reflect and smile at our shared contradictions. Think of him as both your inner challenger and your traveller.

Later in the book, you'll find a reflective session called The Care Compass – a chance to pause and locate yourself in the landscape of care before moving forward. It's not a model to memorise but a moment to orient your own practice.

This is your invitation: to lead with care, to seek balance when the world pulls you to extremes and to hold care for yourself, your people, your results and your values – not as competing demands but as parts of a whole. If this book encourages you to pause, to consider your own journey and to see care as a source of strength rather than softness, it will have served its purpose.

If enough of us lead this way, we will build not only stronger organisations but also stronger societies. Perhaps, together, we can make the world a little better along the way.

Take a breath, find your own rhythm and let's begin.

1
Caring For Results: The Garden Of Growth

A gardener knows that growth is both natural and fragile. Carrots do not flourish just because we demand it of them; they need the right soil, the right care, and the patience of time. Too little water and they wither; too much and they drown. Plant too many seeds too close together and none will thrive. In every choice, the gardener faces the same paradox: results cannot be forced, but neither can they be left to chance.

History shows us the same truth. Empires, companies, even entire movements that pushed too hard, too fast – without nurturing the roots – often collapsed under their own weight. Others, that chose the slower path of care and cultivation, built results that lasted for generations.

Leadership is no different. Numbers on a chart may tell part of the story, but they cannot guarantee it. Results through care require the same wisdom as gardening: to focus, to protect against overload and to create the conditions where growth can take root.

The gardener's wisdom is not in demanding growth but in cultivating it.

FUN FACT: The bondepraktikan

In Sweden, farmers once relied on the Bondepraktikan[1] – a farmer's almanac first published in 1508, combining observational knowledge, early science and folklore to guide agricultural decisions. It mixed superstition with science, offering advice on when to sow seeds and how to predict storms. Not every prediction was reliable, but much of its wisdom was grounded in careful observation.

The lesson for leaders: you can't control the weather – or the markets – but you can prepare wisely.

Leadership in practice: When is 40% growth not enough?

Many years ago, I was presenting quarterly results at a board meeting. Our organisation had just grown more than 40% compared to the previous quarter – surpassing our target by a country mile. As I walked through the presentation, the initial feedback in the room was exceptionally positive. Smiles, nods, even praise. I walked into that room – and out of the presentation – feeling like a star.

During the break, the grey eminence of the board – a senior figure everyone looked up to – came over to me. He congratulated me warmly, and I could tell he meant it. Then he took me aside, looked me straight in the eye, and asked: 'Are you sure that 40% is a good result?'

I was stunned. At first, I thought he hadn't understood, then I realised he was asking something deeper. Had we set the bar too low? Could we have achieved much more – 60%, maybe even 100%? We will never know. That's the paradox of targets: they give us something to aim for, but they can also quietly become ceilings.

If the target had been set too high, the opposite risk appears. A goal that feels unattainable doesn't inspire effort; it discourages it. People stop trying to clear the bar when they believe it is out of reach.

That single question – 'Is 40% really enough?' – changed my perspective forever. It reminded me that results are fragile, not fixed, and that leadership is less about demanding outcomes and more about cultivating them, almost like the gardener. Leaders must not only ask whether ambition is high enough but also whether results are achieved in a way that strengthens rather than weakens people. True care is holding both truths at once: pushing for more, while ensuring that the way we pursue results builds trust and energy, rather than draining it.

Growth is fragile. It requires wisdom.

PARADOX ALERT: Finding the balance

Targets are meant to stretch us, yet they can also hold us back. Set too low, they can leave potential untapped. Set too high, they can crush belief before the first step is even taken.

This is the paradox leaders live with: the same goal that inspires can also intimidate. The same number that creates focus can quietly cap ambition. It is both ladder and ceiling at once.

The challenge – and the responsibility – is to hold that tension with care.

Defining results through care

In this book, **results through care** means achieving outcomes that are not only measurable but also sustainable – results that endure because they are cultivated with attention to people, processes and purpose.

Care in this context is not softness; it is precision. It is the discipline of setting goals that stretch without breaking, creating conditions where teams can thrive and ensuring that progress today does not compromise resilience tomorrow.

Results through care are not demanded; they are nurtured. They require leaders to balance ambition with responsibility, urgency with patience and performance with trust.

In practice, this means leaders must ask not only what results they pursue, but *how* those results are achieved. A target reached at the expense of trust or well-being is not a true result through care – it is a temporary win that erodes the foundation for the future.

FUN FACT: Goodhart's law

Economist Charles Goodhart once observed: 'When a measure becomes a target, it ceases to be a good measure.'[2] This is now known as Goodhart's Law. It explains why chasing numbers alone so often backfires – teachers teaching to the test, salespeople gaming quotas, companies reporting inflated metrics.

It's a reminder that results without care can quickly become hollow. The very act of measuring changes behaviour – which makes how we pursue results just as important as what we measure.

Leadership in practice: When less became more

The company I joined had an impressive portfolio of more than 100 diagnostic tests and a strong analytical platform. On paper, it looked like we had everything we needed to succeed. Yet, despite years of effort, the team had consistently lost out to the bigger players. They went up against the giants again and again – and lost, again and again.

Why was this? Together with the team, I began digging in. We analysed past deals, spoke with customers and listened closely at scientific conferences. What we discovered was sobering: while our portfolio looked broad, about 95% of it overlapped with the competition. Because the bigger companies had an even broader offering, we never stood a chance at winning the big contracts.

What to do? After weeks of analysis and debate, one idea began to emerge. Instead of trying to beat the giants at their own game, what if we looked at the business differently? Where did we have something unique – where no one else could compete? Surprisingly, we found a clear niche: about 5% of our portfolio was ours alone. It wasn't the biggest slice, but it was distinct and it mattered to customers.

At the next sales meeting, I walked in with a large poster of our test portfolio and a black marker pen in my hand. In front of the team, I began crossing out the tests – one after another – until 95% of them were gone. Only a handful remained. The room was silent. You could feel the tension. Could we win with so little? Could 5% be enough?

I was nervous. Cutting away so much felt like a gamble, and I wondered if the team would see it as reckless.

Then something shifted. The salespeople started to lean in. They began to see the value of claiming a space we could truly own. They became experts – not on everything but on the topics that mattered most. Customers noticed.

Then success followed – first in small steps, then with growing momentum. The early wins built confidence, which led to more wins, and soon a positive spiral began. This focus became the turning point. About a year later, it laid the foundation for the growth that would eventually bring me into that boardroom – the one where I presented 40% growth.

It taught me that sometimes care is about choosing focus over breadth – protecting people from chasing unwinnable battles and giving them clarity to excel where they can truly make a difference. Doing less, with care, created far more impact than trying to do it all.

PARADOX ALERT: Narrow to expand

Focus looks like limitation – yet it is often liberation. By stripping away what is unnecessary, we create space for what matters to flourish.

Narrowing choices can expand possibilities. The fewer things we try to do, the better we can become at the things that count. At first it feels like loss, even weakness, but in reality it builds strength.

FUN FACT: Decide to cut

Did you know, the word 'decide' comes from the Latin *decidere*, meaning 'to cut off'?[3] Every decision is, quite literally, an act of focus – cutting off the many in order to make space for the few.

It's a reminder that focus has always carried tension. To decide is not just to choose; it is to let go. In leadership, letting go is often the hardest – and most caring – act of all.

Corporate case stories

Results through care are not confined to personal leadership moments. They can be seen at scale – in companies, communities, even countries. The following stories show how care, when embedded into systems and cultures, creates results that last.

Starbucks: Partners, not employees

When Howard Schultz returned to Starbucks as CEO, the company was in trouble. Stores had expanded too fast and the brand was losing its soul. Schultz doubled down on a simple truth: treat employees as partners, not costs. He restored training, expanded healthcare benefits, even to part-timers, and relaunched stock options.[4]

Investors balked at the expense, but employees responded with loyalty and ownership. Baristas who once saw themselves as temporary staff began calling themselves 'partners' with pride. The company not only rebounded but built a culture that became its competitive moat. Care here was not soft; it was structural – building results by giving people dignity and belonging.

3M: The Post-It almost didn't happen

3M's famous '15% time' gave employees the freedom to experiment, but freedom alone is not enough. Care is what kept fragile ideas alive long enough to prove their worth.

When Art Fry pitched his idea of using Spencer Silver's unusual adhesive for bookmarks, it was brushed off as 'a solution without a problem'.[5] Instead of shutting it down, Fry was given room to test. He handed out samples across the company, and soon colleagues were hooked.

The Post-It note – once a near-reject – became a billion-dollar product. It shows that unlikely seeds can grow, but only if leaders create an environment that protects early shoots rather than pulling them out too soon. Care in this case was protection – guarding fragile ideas until they had a chance to prove themselves.

Toyota: Stopping the line to improve the system

At Toyota, the philosophy of *kaizen* – continuous improvement – is lived daily. On the assembly line, any worker can pull the cord to stop production if they see a problem.[6] Instead of punishment, stopping the line is seen as care: for quality, for colleagues, for customers.

The interruptions are frequent, but they are not failures, they are the gardener's daily watering. Thousands of small acts of care, compounded over time, have made Toyota one of the most consistently excellent carmakers in the world. Results, here, are not squeezed out through pressure – they are cultivated through care.

Community health workers: Care that scales

In parts of Africa, countries such as Rwanda and Ethiopia faced staggering health challenges: high child mortality, mothers dying in childbirth, villages with little or no access to clinics. The solution was not massive hospitals or foreign aid parachuted in – it was local care.

Governments began training women from local communities as health workers. They were given basic medical training, simple equipment and the mandate to care for their neighbours. These women weren't outsiders; they were trusted members of the village.

The results were transformative. Vaccination rates soared, deaths in childbirth plummeted and communities began to trust the health system in a new way.[7] Care here was not abstract – it was personal, delivered face-to-face, neighbour to neighbour. Because it was rooted in trust, it scaled in ways that top-down programmes never could.

The lesson

Whether in a global company, a factory floor or a rural village, the lesson is the same: care is not separate from results, it is the very condition that makes results possible. What looks like extra cost, slowing down or narrowing focus often turns out to be the soil where lasting growth takes root.

PARADOX ALERT: Slow down to speed up

Care can look like slowing down, yet it is often the fastest way forward.

Stopping an assembly line, investing in employee benefits or focusing on just a handful of health workers in a village may seem like delays, costs or limitations, but over time, these very acts of care are what create results that scale, endure and multiply.

What feels like holding back is often what unlocks lasting momentum.

Insights from thinkers

Results through care are not only found in lived leadership moments, they are also echoed in decades of research and practice.

- **Jim Collins: Level 5 leaders** – In *Good to Great,* Collins described 'Level 5 leaders' as those who combine humility with fierce resolve.[8] They don't lead through ego or pressure but by creating conditions where others can succeed. This shows us that enduring results are not built on charisma but on disciplined care.

- **Kouzes and Posner: Enabling others to act** – In *The Leadership Challenge,* Kouzes and Posner emphasise enabling others to act as a cornerstone of leadership.[9] Leaders who build trust, strengthen others and share responsibility often unlock far greater performance than those who try to control outcomes directly. Care here is not a side note; it is the multiplier of results.

- **Peter Drucker and W. Edwards Deming: Purpose and constancy** – Drucker reminded us that 'the purpose of business is to create a customer'.[10] Deming stressed constancy of purpose – staying true to quality over the long term.[11] Both point to the same truth: results without care for meaning and continuity are temporary at best. Leaders must ask not just what results they chase but whose lives are improved by them and whether those gains endure.

- **Teresa Amabile and Steven Kramer: The progress principle** – Harvard's Teresa Amabile and Steven Kramer showed that the strongest driver of creative performance isn't pressure but progress on meaningful work.[12] Even small wins, when recognised, build momentum and motivation. Care here is attention to meaning – helping people see that their work contributes to something that matters.

- **Nelson Mandela: Resilience through care –** Mandela showed that even in politics – where results are often measured in raw power – care can be the deciding factor. After 27 years in prison, he emerged not with vengeance but with a commitment to reconciliation. He knew that pushing too hard for quick wins could fracture South Africa beyond repair. By combining firmness with compassion, he built results that lasted longer than any single election cycle.[13]

Together, these voices echo what the personal stories have already revealed: results without care can dazzle in the moment but rarely endure. Sustainable performance comes from balance – ambition with humility, pressure with trust, short-term gains with long-term meaning and, above all, resilience through care.

Care is all around: Understated care for results

Care doesn't always show up as strategy documents or bold decisions. More often, it lives in the smallest of actions – the ones that make results possible but rarely make the headlines.

In sports, the goalscorer often takes the spotlight, but seasoned players know that the real magic lies in the assist – the perfectly timed pass, the run that draws defenders away, the decision to put the team's success above personal glory. Care here is choosing to step back so someone else can step forward. The result is not just a win on the scoreboard but a culture where trust compounds into championships.

In healthcare, nurses routinely double-check charts, doses and instructions with one another. To an outsider, it might look like a small pause or even inefficiency, but it is care at its most disciplined – the safeguard that prevents errors, protects patients and literally saves lives. These micro-acts of care, invisible to most, are what transform complex systems into places where people can trust the outcome.

In organisations, too, the pattern holds. A colleague who shares credit, a leader who takes an extra minute to explain the 'why', a team that pauses to review lessons learnt – these may look small in the moment but they create the conditions for resilience and results that last.

Care for results, then, is all around us. It isn't always dramatic; it is often quiet, disciplined and deeply human – the hidden force that makes performance sustainable.

FUN FACT: Surgical checklists

When the World Health Organization introduced surgical safety checklists – simple tools to help doctors and nurses pause and confirm key steps – post-surgery complications dropped by more than one-third worldwide.[14] A few seconds of structured care saved thousands of lives.

These small acts show how care multiplies into results, but they also raise a harder question: If care is so powerful, why do leaders so often overlook it – or even design systems that work against it? That is the hypothesis we need to challenge.

Challenge the hypothesis

When we talk about results, we often assume we know what 'good' looks like. Growth. Bigger numbers. More of everything. When we link results to care, it can be tempting to claim that care automatically produces better outcomes, but does it?

The uncomfortable truth is that sometimes results do come from pressure, shortcuts or even neglect. Companies have hit record profits while exploiting people. Leaders have hit targets by burning out teams. Nations have shown dazzling growth numbers while degrading their environments. Even in our own leadership stories, we can mistake short-term spikes for long-term progress.

If we're honest, care is not always the fastest way to visible results. It can feel slower, messier and harder to measure. That is the paradox: the very thing that sustains performance over time can look, in the moment, like it's holding us back.

We must challenge ourselves:

- Are we celebrating numbers that flatter us but hide fragility?
- Are we building systems that reward ambition but quietly punish care?
- Are we pruning enough or chasing growth for its own sake?

Sustainable results demand this self-criticism. Without it, we risk telling ourselves a comfortable story about care – when, in fact, care without courage can drift into complacency, and results without care can collapse just as quickly as they rise.

PARADOX ALERT: The strength in care

Care can look like weakness in the short run – slower decisions, tougher conversations, smaller numbers on the next report. Yet it is exactly this patience and discipline that makes results endure.

Neglect and pressure often deliver the flashiest results fastest, but care, though quieter and slower, is what allows growth to last.

When care for results is missing

It is tempting to believe that results will always speak for themselves. History shows us the opposite: when care for results is missing, the numbers may rise in the short term while the foundations quietly erode.

Think of the global financial crisis of 2008.[15] Banks reported record profits while designing products so complex even their own leaders couldn't explain them. Growth looked dazzling – until it collapsed, taking trust in institutions with it. Results without care became fragility disguised as success.

The same dynamic plays out in corporate life. In the obsession with quarterly targets, some leaders resort to 'stuffing the channel'[16] – pushing excess product into customer or distributor warehouses at the end of a quarter. The numbers look great on paper, bonuses are paid and celebrations are held, but the next quarter begins in deficit, credibility erodes and relationships fray. Careless results are not just unsustainable, they are also self-destructive.

Sometimes the absence of care carries an even greater cost to trust. Consider Dieselgate:[17] Volkswagen hit its emissions targets on paper, thanks to software designed to cheat regulatory tests. For years, sales boomed and the company was celebrated as a green leader. When the truth emerged, the reputational collapse cost billions, shook an entire industry and eroded public faith in corporate responsibility. The numbers had been impressive – but they were a lie.

Here lies the paradox: the brighter the numbers shine, the easier it is to miss the cracks beneath them. Success, when stripped of care, becomes its own disguise – until the collapse makes the truth impossible to ignore.

The warning is clear: care is not the opposite of results, it is the safeguard of results. When care is missing, what looks like growth today often becomes tomorrow's collapse.

Next horizon: Lasting care

The future of results will not be defined by speed alone but by depth. For too long, success has been measured in quarterly gains, short-term wins and numbers that dazzle but do not last. The next horizon of leadership demands a different lens: results that strengthen rather than exhaust, endure rather than evaporate.

This means asking harder questions:

- What kind of growth are we creating – and for whom?

- Are we producing outcomes that can be sustained when leadership changes hands, when markets shift or when crises hit?
- Are we leaving behind systems and cultures that can keep delivering, even without us at the helm?

It also means exploring new measures of success. Lifetime value, total cost of ownership, employee well-being, carbon footprint – these are not 'soft' metrics but future-facing ones. They show whether today's wins will still look like wins in ten years' time.

The leaders who embrace this horizon will see results not just as achievements but as legacies. They will ask not only how fast did we grow this quarter but did we create loyalty that endures? Did we reduce waste that saves costs for years? Did we leave people stronger than before? They will treat numbers as milestones, not finish lines. They will understand that care is not a brake on ambition but the very condition that makes ambition possible over the long term.

The next horizon is clear: results that last are results infused with care. Anything less risks collapsing under its own weight.

The leaders of the future won't be remembered for the records they broke in a quarter but for the foundations they built to last a generation.

Summary

We've reached the end of the first chapter. I want to pause with you here and reflect on what we have learnt.

Reflection questions

- Have you ever celebrated results that later turned out to be fragile? Through the lens of care for results, how did you feel when the cracks began to show? How did your team respond?
- Can you recall a time when hitting a target felt hollow, when the numbers said 'success' but your gut told you otherwise? What conversations followed and what stayed unsaid?
- Have you ever seen results come at the expense of people's well-being? How did that affect the trust, energy or culture around you?
- Think of a moment when someone challenged the definition of success in your team. How did it change the atmosphere in the room: relief, resistance or reflection?
- What would it take for you, today, to measure results not only by the numbers but also by the resilience and meaning they create? If you did, how might others react?

Leadership learnings

- Results without care may deliver speed but they rarely deliver strength.
- Growth is not proof of success; sometimes it is evidence of fragility.
- Treat targets with caution: a number can be both a compass and a cage.
- Celebrating results is easy; questioning them requires courage.
- The true test of leadership is not achieving results in your presence but ensuring they continue in your absence. This is why care for results is never about lowering the bar – it is about lifting the meaning of the bar.

Ask from the author

Results may feel like familiar territory, but I invite you to rethink what they mean. It is tempting to celebrate quick wins, high growth rates or quarterly spikes, but care for results asks us to look deeper. Are these achievements sustainable, meaningful and aligned with the purpose we claim to serve?

Remember, results that dazzle without care rarely last. Pause and ask yourself which of your goals measure vanity and which measure vitality? Which key performance indicators (KPIs) celebrate activity and which capture real progress?

Dare to be the voice in the room that challenges easy victories. Be the leader who asks: Is this truly success or just the illusion of it?

Leadership is not about proving success once. It is about ensuring it can endure, season after season.

2

Caring About People: A Campfire For Hearts And Minds

Long before dashboards and KPIs, people measured progress by something simpler: gathering around a fire at the end of the day. The campfire wasn't just warmth or light – it was where stories were told, food was shared and trust was built.

What makes the campfire so powerful is its dual nature. It invites the group together, creating a sense of belonging, yet it also respects the individual. You can sit quietly, gaze into the flames and still feel part of something larger. Around the fire, introverts and extroverts alike can find their place.

Leadership that cares for people works the same way. It is not only about driving tasks forward but creating spaces where people feel safe to speak, or safe simply to be. It is noticing when someone needs to step back and when another is ready to step in.

I've seen it myself. In teams where pressure was high, a simple pause – time set aside to listen and connect – often reignited trust more effectively than any metric. Like a fire, care needs tending: feeding it with attention, stoking it with honesty and sometimes clearing the ashes of past mistakes so new warmth can emerge.

Results matter but people endure. The leaders who understand this don't just manage performance; they gather their teams around a fire that keeps both heart and mind alive. Which is why, in this book, I define care for people not as a soft afterthought but as the very soil in which trust, performance and resilience grow.

FUN FACT: Fire and human connection

Anthropologists have found that conversations around campfires are measurably different from those in daylight. At the fire, people are more likely to share stories, reflect on the past and plan for the future. One study even suggested that firelight extended the length and depth of conversations in early human groups – making the campfire not just a source of warmth but a cradle of culture, trust and collaboration.[18]

Leadership in practice: From dashboards to trust

As leaders, we often focus on results. Performance dashboards, KPIs and quarterly targets dominate our attention – and rightly so. Results matter. They are the brain of the organisation, the measures of whether or not our strategies are working.

While this is true, sustainable performance only happens when the brain of the organisation connects with the hearts of its people. Numbers alone cannot sustain growth; people's belief, energy and trust are what keep it alive.

One lesson sits very strongly with me from when I took over a leadership team in a new country. On paper, everything looked perfect: KPIs were all green and reports painted a picture of smooth sailing. In reality, the business was failing. Something didn't add up.

In team meetings, emotions were absent. No one talked about frustrations, fears or even pride – everything was flattened into dashboards. I remember one department presenting a full set of green KPIs while the company as a whole was far from hitting its key targets. The message was clear: as long as my numbers are fine, I'm fine. It wasn't care for the whole, it was self-preservation dressed up as success.

That was the moment I actually blew a fuse – something that is rare for me. I couldn't reconcile the 'all green' picture with the reality I knew we were facing. If we couldn't even name the problems, how could we ever solve them? That anger became the spark to start asking harder questions.

From then on, I began asking two questions, again and again, in different settings – with the leadership team, in one-on-ones and even in wider gatherings:

1. Where are we really heading?
2. What did we actually celebrate?

The first created silence – the uncomfortable kind that reveals truth. The second exposed a paradox: we were celebrating milestones that didn't matter, applauding ourselves while the ship was slowly sinking. Were we caring for people or only for ourselves, avoiding the hard truths?

Slowly, things shifted. It began in the leadership team. We moved away from dashboards and talked about purpose – why we were there and what we owed each other. Care meant daring to open up, not just about results but also about the struggles behind them.

As trust grew, the circles widened. Extended teams got involved. People began offering help outside their silos, not because it was mandated but because they felt safe to do so. Psychological safety was no longer a buzzword – it lived in the way people challenged, supported and shared burdens.

Even our metrics evolved. We talked openly about why measures exist – and why a red KPI can be more valuable than a green one, because it reveals what needs attention. Later, we moved from KPIs to OKRs: objectives and key results that were ambitious by design. Hitting 80% could mean real success if the bar was high enough. This only worked because engagement and trust had been built. Without care, ambitious OKRs would have crushed instead of inspired.

In time, the results followed. Dashboards began to tell a different story – one that matched the reality we could feel in the room. The lesson stayed with me: you can run on green KPIs for a while, but without care, green eventually turns red. With care, results don't just improve, they endure.

That insight – that care changes not only how people feel but how results themselves are defined and pursued – set the stage for what came next.

FUN FACT: The canary in the coal mine

Before modern sensors, miners carried canaries underground to detect toxic gases. The birds often looked fine until suddenly collapsing – a stark early warning that danger was already present.[19]

Organisations have their own 'canaries'. A dashboard may glow green, but if people don't feel safe to speak up, problems are already in the air. The real question for leaders is this: Do you know who your canary is, and how quickly would you notice if it stopped singing?

PARADOX ALERT: The illusion of care

In many organisations, green dashboards are celebrated as signs of success, yet true care sometimes shows up in red. A red KPI can signal that people feel safe enough to speak the truth, to raise risks and to admit when things aren't working. While green can hide silence or fear, red can reveal honesty, trust and the chance to improve. Sometimes the bravest leaders are the ones who celebrate red – because it means people trust them enough not to fake green.

While green dashboards and polished feedback can look like care, they can also hide its absence. Real care is not about appearances; it is about creating an environment where people feel safe enough to speak the truth. What looks like strength – flawless results and perfect harmony – may in fact be fragility. True care embraces the messy conversations that keep a team alive.

Defining care for people

When we talk about **care for people**, it is easy to confuse it with being nice, friendly or avoiding conflict. Care in leadership is not about comfort; it is about commitment.

In this book, I define care for people as the commitment to create conditions where individuals feel safe, valued and trusted – not just as employees but as human beings. True care is never about appearances or 'green dashboards'; it is about creating spaces where voices are heard, where people can admit mistakes without fear and where contributions are recognised for their real worth.

Research in organisational psychology has shown again and again that people perform at their best when they feel psychologically safe. Amy Edmondson's work demonstrates that high-performing teams thrive not because they eliminate errors but because they trust each other enough to speak up about them.[20] This is care in action: it is not the absence of failure but the presence of trust.

Care for people also means being willing to challenge. It is not indulgence or blind support but the courage to address hard truths, to give feedback that helps someone grow and to show consistency, even under pressure. Without it, results may look strong in the short term but they lack roots. With it, teams can withstand setbacks, find energy in each other and sustain performance in ways that endure.

Sometimes, the difference between a culture that looks healthy on the surface and one that truly cares is revealed in the smallest cracks – when numbers are green but people's hearts are not. That's where the second story begins.

Leadership in practice: Feedback vs. care

Giving feedback – especially the negative kind – has always been one of my biggest development areas as a leader. I like to think of myself as self-aware and genuinely engaged in helping people grow, yet even with that intent it's been surprisingly hard to change old habits.

For a long time, feedback conversations drained me. I would rehearse them in my head, searching for the perfect words – not too harsh, not too vague – only to end up postponing them. It wasn't that I didn't care; quite the opposite. I cared so much that I didn't want to hurt people. I mistook comfort for kindness.

One example still stands out. A talented manager on my team consistently underdelivered in collaboration. Smart, capable but increasingly isolated. I knew it, others knew it – yet I kept softening my messages, telling myself I was 'being supportive'. Deep down, I was avoiding discomfort – for both of us. Months later, she was frustrated, I was frustrated, and the team was suffering. My silence hadn't protected her; it had held her back.

What finally broke the pattern was a development centre I attended as an observer. My task was to watch participants and give feedback at the end of each exercise. The strange thing was: I had no hesitation there. I was clear, direct, even generous with my observations. Participants thanked me – even for the tough parts – because they could feel my intent: I wanted them to grow.

Driving home afterwards, I asked myself a hard question: Why can I be brave with strangers and hesitant with my own people?

That question stayed with me. Over time, I realised I'd been confusing care with protection. Real care is not shielding people from the truth – it's trusting them enough to handle it. When I shifted that mindset, feedback transformed. It was no longer about pointing out flaws but about unlocking potential.

One conversation stands out from that turning point. I sat down with a colleague and said, 'I've realised I haven't been fair to you. I've seen things that could help you grow, but I've held back because I didn't want to discourage you. That was my mistake. You deserve honesty, not comfort.'

We talked openly for an hour. It was raw, but something changed. She later told me it was the most meaningful feedback she'd ever received – not because it was easy, but because it was real.

That day taught me that care without truth is sentimentality and truth without care is brutality, but when the two meet, growth becomes possible.

PARADOX ALERT: The balance of warmth and edge

Caring about people is not the same as making them comfortable. Too little care creates fear as people hold back, hide mistakes and protect themselves. Too much care – expressed as protection from discomfort – can quietly limit growth.

Leaders who shield their people from hard truths may believe they are showing empathy, but in reality, they are denying them the opportunity to stretch, stumble and evolve. Care sometimes demands discomfort.

True care has both warmth and edge. It listens deeply but it also challenges bravely. It builds trust not by avoiding tension but by holding it with respect. A leader who only comforts risks creates dependency. A leader who only challenges risks creates fear. Sustainable performance – and genuine human growth – live in the space where both meet.

Corporate case stories

Care for people isn't just a philosophy, it plays out in boardrooms, on shop floors and in communities. The question is never if care matters but how it is embedded: in the individual, the culture, the system. The evidence is striking: where care is present, performance follows; where it is absent, cracks quickly appear.

Google's Project Oxygen: Coaching as the core of leadership

When Google set out to define what made great managers, they expected technical expertise to top the list. Instead, the number-one factor was coaching: leaders who supported development, gave feedback and created space for growth.[21] Care turned out to be the true differentiator.

Satya Nadella at Microsoft: Leading with empathy

When Nadella took over Microsoft, the company was seen as rigid and combative. He reframed the culture around a growth mindset and empathy. Leaders were encouraged to ask questions, listen deeply and coach rather than command.[22] This human shift revitalised innovation and collaboration across the company.

Mondragon Cooperative: Shared ownership as care

In the Basque region of Spain, a small group of workers in the 1950s faced poverty and unemployment in the aftermath of war. Instead of waiting for outside rescue, they built their own system: the Mondragon Cooperative. From the start, care was embedded, not as charity but as structure – employees became owners. Profits were shared, wage gaps were capped and decisions were made democratically.[23]

Over the decades, Mondragon grew into a federation of more than ninety cooperatives with over 70,000 employees worldwide. Through recessions and global crises, it proved remarkably resilient, often outperforming traditional corporations. The reason? People did not feel like cogs in a machine. They felt like partners in a shared future.

Uber's early culture: When care is missing

At the height of its early success, Uber became a case study in what happens when care is absent.[24] Aggression was rewarded, collaboration was dismissed and fear ran high. The short-term results were undeniable but the long-term costs were devastating: lawsuits, resignations, reputational damage and a painful rebuilding process. A reminder that care is not optional, it is foundational.

The lesson

Together, these stories paint a clear pattern: care multiplies results, neglect erodes them. Whether it comes through coaching, empathy, shared ownership or simply the absence of fear, care is not a 'soft' extra – it is the foundation on which performance and resilience are built.

Here's are some harder questions:

- Where in your own system is care visible, and where is it missing?
- Which of your practices lift people up and which quietly push them down?

Every leader, every team, every organisation leaves a trail of how it treats people. The true test of leadership is whether that trail builds trust – or leaves scars.

Insights from thinkers

- **Amy Edmondson: Trust equals performance –** We touched on the work of Harvard professor Amy Edmondson earlier in this chapter, and it deserves to be revisited. Her research on psychological safety has reshaped our understanding of what truly drives performance – not the absence of mistakes but the presence of trust. Teams that feel safe enough to speak up, question and admit errors learn faster and achieve more. Carc makes that honesty possible.

  Neuroscience supports what Edmondson found. When people feel threatened or judged, the brain's amygdala triggers a stress response, shutting down creativity and collaboration. When they feel trusted and valued, the prefrontal cortex engages – the part of the brain responsible for empathy, reasoning and innovation. In short: care changes not only culture but also chemistry.[25]

- **Daniel Goleman: Emotional intelligence as structured care** – Goleman's work on emotional intelligence adds another layer. His research shows that leaders who combine self-awareness, empathy and self-regulation consistently outperform those who rely on authority or drive alone.[26] Emotional intelligence, at its core, is structured care – the discipline of understanding both yourself and others.

- **Aristotle: Classic leadership models** – Long before neuroscience and leadership models, Aristotle described virtue as 'the mean between extremes', a foundational concept in ethical philosophy.[27] That idea captures the paradox we've explored throughout this chapter – real care lives between softness and toughness, warmth and edge. Leadership, in that sense, is not about choosing one over the other but about mastering the balance between them.

- **Mary Parker Follett: Empowerment at the core** – Nearly two millennia later, Follett reframed leadership not as command but as empowerment. 'The test of a leader,' she wrote, 'is not how much power you have, but how much power you give to others.'[28] Few sentences capture the spirit of care more precisely.

- **Gallup: A modern take** – Modern data reinforces what these thinkers intuited. Gallup found that employees who feel genuinely cared for are more engaged, productive and loyal.[29] Recognition and belonging are not sentimental, they are strategic.

Across centuries and disciplines, the conclusion remains the same:

- Psychology shows that care builds safety.
- Neuroscience shows that safety enables learning.
- Philosophy reminds us that virtue lies in balance.
- Leadership research proves that balance sustains results.

These insights remind us that care is both ancient and evolving – a principle that has guided human groups since long before organisations existed. What truly brings it to life is not research or philosophy but daily practice. It's in the moments where leaders pause, listen and act with intention.

You don't need to be a CEO or team manager to see it. Care is everywhere – in the way people open space for one another. It is not the opposite of performance, care is its most reliable foundation.

Care is all around: Daily practice

In some companies, teams begin meetings with a simple check-in round. Each person shares how they're arriving – tired, hopeful, worried, energised. It takes just a few minutes, but it changes the room. Suddenly, people are not just roles or resources; they're human beings.

In another organisation, a manager keeps a 'recognition wall' in the break area. Anyone can post a note of appreciation – small, specific, personal. Over time, that wall has become a quiet heartbeat of the culture, a reminder that being seen matters as much as being right.

In Japan, many factories hold a brief morning ceremony before the workday begins. Teams stand together, stretch and bow to each other – a gesture of respect that says: we're in this together. It's not performance, it's belonging, made visible.

Sports teams have their own rituals. When a player has a bad game, teammates don't only analyse performance – they put an arm around a shoulder, reminding each other that the jersey represents community, not just output. In one elite football club, players are asked after each match: Who lifted you today? It reframes success from individual stats to shared support.

In healthcare, where the stakes are literally life and death, care shows up in small but profound ways. In one hospital system, nurses end every shift with a brief 'gratitude circle'. Each person calls out one colleague for something they appreciated that day – big or small. It began as an experiment and spread quietly across departments. The result wasn't only higher morale but fewer reported errors. When people feel seen, they pay more attention – to each other and to their work.

Even in digital-first companies, care finds new forms. Some teams have introduced 'camera-off days', allowing people to recharge without pressure to perform visually. Others send 'wellness pings' instead of status checks – one-line questions such as: How are you showing up today? It's a reminder that performance starts with presence.

Care is not a leadership style, it's a daily practice. It lives in check-ins, acknowledgements and honest conversations. It's the quiet voice that says, 'I see you, I value you and I'm here with you, even when things are hard.'

Wherever hearts and minds meet – around a campfire, a factory floor, a Zoom call or a hospital corridor – care is already at work.

Challenge the hypothesis

In this chapter, we've argued that caring for people is not a distraction from results but a foundation for them. Let's pause and ask: Is this actually true? If so, why? What would speak against it?

The counterargument is tempting: history is full of leaders who drove performance without much visible care. Fear can sharpen focus, pressure can push people past what they thought possible, competition can fuel innovation – there's truth in that. No care at all – or artificial care that is really manipulation dressed up as kindness – can seem more effective in the short term than genuine investment in people. We've all seen examples: a company launching a 'wellness programme' to tick a box while quietly demanding unsustainable hours, or a leader sugarcoating bad news rather than facing people with honesty. That isn't care, it's camouflage.

Why insist that care for people is essential? Because while fear and pressure may deliver short-term sprints, they rarely sustain the marathon. The data is consistent: environments built on neglect, intimidation or shallow care burn out their people, bleed talent and stifle creativity. What looks like efficiency in the moment often reveals itself as fragility over time.

To those who argue that people are replaceable: history tells another story. Yes, you can burn through people like fuel but eventually the fire consumes the organisation too. The most successful companies, communities and even nations do not endure because they treat people as expendable but because they build systems that make people want to stay, contribute and innovate. Fear can command obedience; only care inspires commitment.

PARADOX ALERT: Fear burns bright, then burns out

History offers plenty of proof that fear can deliver results, but only for a while. The Soviet Union drove astonishing industrial output under Stalin,[30] but it came at the cost of human lives, innovation and ultimately the system itself. Fear produced compliance, but it also planted the seeds of collapse.

Fear can ignite a blaze, but it consumes everything in its path. Care may feel slower, but it fuels growth that lasts.

What looks like control in the short term often hides deep fragility underneath.

When care is missing

When care is missing, people stop giving their best ideas first. They say less in meetings, share less between departments and invest less of themselves in the work. Performance may remain – for a while – but energy and ownership fade. The organisation becomes efficient but lifeless, like a machine running smoothly without warmth.

In today's workplaces, this often shows up as 'quiet quitting'.[31] People still meet expectations, but only just. They protect their boundaries not out of balance but out of disappointment – doing what's required, not what they're capable of. It's not rebellion; it's resignation.

Others go the opposite way – they overperform to survive. They fill every gap, answer every email, stay late, smile through exhaustion. It looks like commitment but it's self-protection. Without care, even excellence can become armour.

Then there's cynicism, the slow corrosion of belief. When people no longer trust that their leaders mean what they say, they stop believing their own effort matters. That's when humour turns sarcastic, meetings go quiet and real innovation disappears.

Sometimes, the problem isn't too little care – but care in name only. Organisations launch well-being programmes, empathy workshops or 'pulse surveys' that signal care but never change the underlying behaviour. This performative care may look compassionate, but people sense the gap between message and reality. It breeds the very disengagement it aims to prevent.

At first, results might not change much. In fact, they sometimes improve – at least on paper – but it's a false peak. Without real care, people disconnect emotionally long before they walk out physically. The cost is hidden – creativity, trust and long-term resilience – until suddenly it isn't.

The absence of care doesn't always break a system; it drains it. Slowly, quietly, until there's nothing left to give.

The inverse is also true: the moment care re-enters – when someone listens, thanks or tells the truth – life begins to return. The heartbeat comes back.

Fear may silence people but indifference makes them disappear. Leadership without care is, in the end, leadership without followers.

Next horizon: Building leadership through trust

The question now is not whether care matters but whether it can survive the forces reshaping work.

In the years ahead, organisations will face a choice. Some will double down on control – relying on data, AI and tighter performance systems to drive efficiency. It will seem rational, even necessary, but reducing people to dashboards risks repeating the same mistake that once eroded trust. Others will take a different path – one that treats empowerment not as risk but as strength. They'll build systems where care scales, where autonomy and accountability coexist and where technology supports instead of replaces human judgement. These organisations will see that speed and empathy are not opposites – that adaptability grows from trust, not fear.

History moves like a pendulum. Uncertainty often drives leaders back to control. Yet every enduring era – from the cooperative movements of the 1950s to today's agile revolutions – has rediscovered the same truth: sustainable success is built on inclusion, trust and care.

The next horizon of leadership belongs to those who blend clarity with freedom – who know that care isn't softness but strength, that empowerment isn't the absence of direction but the multiplication of purpose. The challenge ahead is not to choose between people and performance but to design systems where one depends on the other.

The real test of leadership will not be how much control we exert but how much trust we enable. That is where we turn next: from caring for people to caring for the system – ensuring that the structures we build are capable of caring back.

Summary

Take a moment to think about what you have learnt in this chapter.

Reflection questions

- What signals tell you that people in your team feel truly safe? What signals might suggest the opposite?

- How do you currently define care in your leadership? How would your team describe it?
- What does fear look like in your culture today? How is it shaping the conversations you're *not* having?
- If you measured trust as carefully as performance, what patterns would you start to see?
- Whose voice isn't being heard right now? What could you do this week to invite it in?
- How do you personally balance honesty and empathy when giving feedback?
- When you think about your own 'campfire' of leadership, what kind of space are you creating for others to gather around?
- What one daily or weekly ritual could you introduce that makes care visible and repeatable in your team?

Leadership learnings

- Care is a performance strategy. It's not softness; it's the foundation that allows people to think clearly, speak truthfully and act bravely.
- Safety and challenge go hand in hand. People grow most where trust allows discomfort to be used for learning, not fear.

- Feedback is fuel. It builds capability when it's given with the intent to help, not to judge.
- Red is not failure, it's information. When people can show the truth, the team starts to solve what really matters.
- Warmth needs edge. Empathy without courage becomes comfort; courage without empathy becomes control. The art is holding both.
- Culture is built in the moments between meetings. Small rituals – recognition, check-ins, genuine curiosity – show what your leadership truly values.
- The best leaders connect hearts and minds. They balance results with relationships, turning performance into purpose.

Ask from the author

Before you move on to the next chapter, pause for a moment. Think of one person – just one – who would benefit if you led with a little more care this week. It could be someone you've avoided giving feedback to, a colleague who's gone quiet or a team that feels stuck in 'green KPI' comfort.

Your task is simple. Create one real moment of care. Ask the harder question, offer honest feedback, recognise an effort that usually goes unseen.

Care doesn't need a programme or a speech. It needs presence, courage and consistency.

If every leader did that once a week, cultures would change faster than any transformation plan ever could. That's how leadership grows – one honest act of care at a time.

3

Caring About Yourself: Fuel, Not Fire

Along many coastlines, you'll find rows of stones or concrete arms stretching into the sea – breakwaters built to protect the shore. They don't stop the tide or silence the waves; they simply absorb some of the impact, giving the land behind them a chance to breathe. Self-care works the same way. It doesn't eliminate pressure or prevent storms; it creates the structures that allow you to withstand them.

For me, those structures began as habits – sleep, movement, reflection, honest conversations. For others, they might look different: boundaries, nature, learning, prayer, creativity. The shape doesn't matter as much as the purpose – to take the first shock, so that what truly matters stays intact.

Without breakwaters, even a calm sea will eventually erode the shore. Without self-care, even meaningful work will grind down the spirit that gives it purpose.

Building your breakwaters takes time, patience and humility. You have to learn your own currents – where you're most exposed, where the storms hit hardest – and then you build accordingly.

Leadership, like the ocean, will always have tides. The question isn't whether the waves will come – they will. The question is whether you've built the structures that let you stay standing when they do.

Self-care builds the breakwater; shared care turns it into a harbour – a place where others can find calm and courage too.

FUN FACT: Nature's engineers

Along some coastlines, coral reefs and mangroves act as natural breakwaters, reducing wave energy by up to 97%.[32] They don't fight the ocean; they dance with it.

Our nervous systems work in the same way: calm, connection and recovery soften life's impact far better than sheer force ever could. Real resilience isn't about resisting – it's about responding with grace.

Leadership in practice: My health wake-up call

I still remember waking up early one morning in Istanbul. The plan was simple: squeeze in a workout before a packed day of meetings, but as I laced up my shoes, a wave of vertigo hit me. My body felt heavy, my head was spinning, my energy gone. I'm fine, I told myself – just tired – but the same thing happened again and again. Weeks passed before I admitted I needed help.

When I finally went to the doctor, the truth hit me like a punch to the stomach. She put me on the scale, checked my blood pressure, ran a few tests and then looked me in the eye. Her verdict was blunt: I was overweight, my blood pressure dangerously high, and if I didn't change, I was heading for serious trouble.

I thought I had been coping. In reality, I was running on fumes. At work, I was irritable and short-tempered. At home, I had lost interest in things that usually gave me joy. I wasn't showing up as the leader or the person I aspired to be.

The road back wasn't glamorous – it was gruelling. I committed to ten hours of solid workouts every week. I practised mindful eating, weighing food and measuring my weight, blood pressure and other vital signs daily. I had to step away from one of my passions, whisky tasting, because I couldn't afford the extra calories. It was a series of small sacrifices that often felt like uphill battles.

The beginning was the hardest. Muscles ached, habits resisted and the scale refused to move as quickly as I wanted. There were setbacks – small injuries, fatigue, moments of doubt – but I kept going. Slowly, results started to appear. I felt stronger, lighter, sharper. The clarity and energy I thought I had lost began to return.

Here's the paradox: the sacrifices that once felt painful became sources of strength. What seemed like giving things up turned out to be gaining so much more – presence, resilience and the ability to lead with authenticity again.

That journey taught me a lesson I will never forget. The flight safety instruction says: 'Put on your own oxygen mask before helping others.'[33] I used to dismiss that as cliché, but now I know it's the essence of sustainable leadership.

You can't lead on empty.

Caring for others starts with caring for yourself – not as an act of selfishness but as an act of stewardship. Leadership isn't only about driving outcomes; it's about protecting the energy and clarity that make those outcomes possible.

More than a year later, the work continues, but the challenge has shifted. It's no longer about losing weight; it's about building strength without losing balance. I've had to learn new habits again: adapting workouts, experimenting with nutrition, finding rhythms that sustain rather than strain.

That's the deeper realisation: caring for yourself is never a finished project. It's a lifelong discipline of adaptation – of finding habits that endure while still allowing you to enjoy each day. The goal isn't perfection, it's presence.

Even in cultures that celebrate balance, care still begins within. Systems can encourage it, but only individuals can choose to live it.

PARADOX ALERT: The Nordic balance

Scandinavia is often praised for work–life balance, generous parental leave and short working hours, yet burnout is still common. How can societies with so much focus on balance still struggle?

Caring systems cannot replace individual responsibility. Even in the most supportive environments, leaders must take personal ownership of their resilience. Cultural norms may encourage rest, but unless individuals truly embrace and protect it, the systems are not enough.

The deeper lesson: self-care must always be a partnership. Culture and systems can guide and protect, but ultimately, leaders themselves must commit to their own oxygen. A supportive culture opens the door, but only individuals can choose to walk through it.

Defining care for yourself

Caring for yourself is not self-indulgence, it's self-respect. It's the conscious act of maintaining the physical, emotional and mental capacity to show up as the person and leader you aspire to be.

In this book, I define **care for yourself** as the commitment to protect and renew your own energy so that presence and purpose can endure over time.

It's easy to confuse self-care with comfort: taking breaks, relaxing or rewarding yourself after long hours, but true care is deeper. True care is the discipline of setting boundaries, the courage to rest before you crash and the honesty to admit when you've lost balance.

Caring for yourself follows the same principle elite athletes live by. They don't perform at maximum intensity every day. They train, rest and recover – not because they're weak but because they understand how strength is built.

Leadership is no different. High performance depends on recovery. Pushing harder can yield results for a while, but without renewal, capacity erodes. True resilience is not the ability to keep going endlessly – it's the ability to pause, restore and return stronger.

Caring for yourself is not a solo act either – it's relational. It shapes how you show up for others. When leaders neglect themselves, teams feel it: impatience rises, empathy fades, creativity shrinks. The cost of exhaustion is rarely paid in private; it ripples through the system.

Yet care for self isn't about perfection, it's about rhythm. Energy expands and contracts, focus ebbs and flows, life demands adjustment. The real mastery lies not in avoiding depletion but in learning to notice it early – and to restore before you're forced to recover.

Because the paradox of leadership is this: the more responsibility you hold, the more intentionally you must care for yourself. Without that foundation, even the most capable leaders will eventually run out of oxygen.

FUN FACT: Eat like you lead

Elite athletes don't think about food as reward, they see it as fuel. Every meal is a strategic choice to sustain performance, not a reaction to fatigue. Studies show that Olympic athletes spend as much time planning recovery and nutrition as they do training.[34]

Leaders can learn from that mindset: care for self isn't a reward after effort – it's what makes effort possible.

Leadership in practice: Resilience together

Organisations don't always realise the impact they can have on people's lives. A sudden reorganisation, shifting priorities or endless demands can feel like just another line in a strategy presentation. For individuals, those changes can land like a shockwave – unsettling identity, confidence and even health.

I saw this happen to my wife and partner in crime, Elisabeth – the strongest and most resilient person I know. She had been thriving in a start-up, pouring her energy into building something new, taking on responsibility after responsibility. Then overnight, a reorganisation reshaped her role beyond recognition. It was as if the ground beneath her feet gave way.

The irony was not lost on me. This was around the same time I was finding my own footing again after a difficult health journey. As I began to regain strength, Elisabeth was losing hers. It reminded me that care is rarely synchronised – one moment you're the one being carried, the next you're the one holding steady.

We both stood low during that period, just in different ways. It wasn't only about work; it was about stability, trust and direction. What struck me most was how care – for each other, for what truly mattered – slowly began to rebuild our strength. Step by step, through small moments of encouragement, honesty and shared hope, resilience began to return.

Almost out of nowhere, the farm of our dreams appeared on the market. It seemed impossible – too big, too expensive, too risky. Buying it would mean stretching ourselves beyond comfort, maybe even beyond reason. Yet something about it felt right. It carried something no spreadsheet could measure: hope.

Working the land, learning new skills, fixing what was broken – it all demanded a lot from us. Yet the more we gave, the more alive we felt. That's when I realised: self-care isn't only about rest – it's also about creation. Doing what you love, learning something new, engaging with the world through curiosity and purpose – these things restore energy in ways rest alone never can.

The farm became more than a property. It became a teacher – showing us that resilience grows through both stillness and movement, through both recovery and re-engagement.

That experience reminded me that resilience is not about standing tall at all times. Sometimes it's about being knocked down, admitting the low and then finding a path – often unexpected – that restores strength.

For Elisabeth, and for us together, the farm became that path. For me as a leader, it reinforced a truth:

organisations must remember that people are not just workers; they are whole human beings. If we design systems without care, we risk breaking the very resilience we rely on.

PARADOX ALERT: The productivity trap

After every low, there's an instinct to prove that we're back – to work harder, show results, fill the silence with movement.

I've seen it in myself, in teams and in whole organisations. The more drained we become, the more we tend to double down on productivity. Leaders who are running on empty often compensate with control – more meetings, tighter grip, endless urgency.

Exhaustion rarely heals through effort. The very drive that fuels success can quietly destroy sustainability.

When care disappears, performance becomes self-consuming – efficient in the short term, eroding in the long run.

The real test of leadership is not how hard you can push but how wisely you can pause.

Corporate case stories

If self-care is the foundation of leadership, then organisational care is the architecture. Some companies build it in from the start; others only learn after cracks appear.

These examples show both – moments when structure protected energy and times when speed eroded it.

Google: Mindfulness as cultural infrastructure

Even the most forward-thinking organisations eventually learn that brilliance without balance is unsustainable.

Google's experiment with mindfulness began in 2007 as a side project, not a strategy. Search Inside Yourself was designed to help employees focus better and manage stress, but many dismissed it as soft or unnecessary.

Over time, the data told a different story.[35] Teams that practised mindfulness reported lower stress, higher empathy and improved collaboration. What started as a wellness initiative evolved into cultural infrastructure – reflection built into rhythm.

Microsoft Japan: The four-day work trial

In 2019, Microsoft Japan ran a month-long trial reducing the workweek to four days. Meetings were shortened, decisions were delegated and employees were encouraged to use their Fridays for rest or learning. Productivity jumped by 40%, while energy and satisfaction rose sharply.[36]

The lesson was structural, not symbolic: when systems are designed to protect focus and renewal, performance improves – not in spite of reduced hours, but because of them.

Patagonia: Values into policy

Patagonia's mantra, 'Let My People Go Surfing', is more than a slogan – it's operational philosophy.[37] Flexible work hours, on-site childcare and permission to reconnect with nature aren't perks; they're performance enablers.

The company's culture ties renewal to its environmental mission. Care for people and care for planet are not separate conversations – they are one system.

Médecins Sans Frontières (MSF): Recovery by design

In humanitarian work, intensity is constant and emotional strain unavoidable. MSF embeds recovery into its structure through rotation schedules, mandatory decompression periods, and psychological support between missions.[38] These aren't optional add-ons – they're part of the logistics of care.

In a field that celebrates sacrifice, MSF treats restoration as duty. It's not about heroism; it's about sustainability.

The lesson

Google teaches us that reflection built into rhythm outperforms 'add more hours'. From Microsoft Japan, we learn that design constraints create capacity. Patagonia's story shows that when values and calendars align, energy compounds. Finally, from MSF we learn that in high-intensity work, recovery is logistics, not luxury. Together, these companies reveal a simple truth: culture is not what you write on walls, it's what you schedule, allow and repeat.

High-growth 'crunch' cultures: The burnout loop

Many start-ups and gaming studios have worn 'crunch time' as a badge of honour – marathon coding sessions, midnight launches and relentless speed. The results can look impressive in the short term, but attrition, health costs and creative fatigue always follow.[39]

The pattern is predictable: output spikes, people burn out, replacements arrive and the cycle repeats – until reputation and quality collapse.

If speed comes from sacrifice, the bill arrives with interest.

Whether through mindfulness, redesigned schedules or recovery logistics, these organisations discovered the same thing: sustainable performance is engineered, not improvised.

When care is planned, people don't just endure – they evolve.

Insights from thinkers

Even the most accomplished leaders eventually meet the limits of endurance. Their recoveries remind us that care for self is not weakness – it's leadership in practice.

The following thinkers and change-makers each turned personal collapse into collective learning – proof that individual renewal can reshape entire systems.

- **Dan Harris: Name it to tame it** – When news anchor Dan Harris suffered a panic attack live on air, millions witnessed what most leaders hide – burnout breaking the surface. Instead of retreating, he chose honesty. His openness became advocacy through *10% Happier*, helping others rediscover calm and focus through mindfulness.[40]

  His story proved that recovery often begins the moment we stop pretending we're fine. We need to normalise check-ins and use honest language about stress, making 'I'm at capacity' sayable.

- **Jacinda Ardern: Steward the tank** – When New Zealand's Prime Minister resigned in 2023, she said that she had no longer enough in the tank to do the job justice.[41]

Her candour reframed leadership not as endless endurance but as stewardship of energy. It was a global moment of grace – proof that stepping back can be an act of integrity, not failure.

We need to define the red lines and recovery plans before we need them.

- **Arianna Huffington: Redefine success –** At the height of her career, Arianna Huffington collapsed from exhaustion, fracturing her cheekbone on her desk. That fall forced her to question the meaning of success itself. She later founded Thrive Global, built on the conviction that well-being is not a perk but infrastructure.[42]

  Her story shows how personal collapse can become a blueprint for collective change. Well-being isn't a perk; it's performance infrastructure.

- **James Clear: Tiny habits, durable change –** Author and researcher James Clear distilled behaviour change into one insight: small habits compound.[43] Sustainable growth doesn't come from intensity but from identity-based consistency. His work shows that care for self isn't a grand gesture – it's the quiet alignment of daily actions with who you want to become.

- We learn that sustainability beats intensity – building streaks, not sprints.

Each of these stories carries the same current: care begins as a private choice but matures into a public responsibility. When leaders choose honesty over image, they expand what's possible for everyone around them – turning vulnerability into infrastructure.

These stories – from boardrooms to breakpoints – reveal that care is both personal and structural, inner and outer.

Transformation only begins when insight becomes action, so before turning the page, pause for a moment. Shift the lens from them to you. Where in your own leadership rhythm could care move from intention to design?

Care is all around: The everyday architects of renewal

Across the globe, there are places where people live longer, healthier and more connected lives – the so-called Blue Zones.[44] From Okinawa in Japan to Sardinia in Italy and Nicoya in Costa Rica, the secret isn't hidden in medicine or technology, it's found in rhythm. They move naturally, eat simply, stay connected and live with purpose. Care for self isn't a solo project – it's a shared culture of balance.

Closer to home, Scandinavia offers its own quiet ritual: *fika*.[45] It looks like a coffee break but it's a structured social pause, supporting connection, recovery and informal communication – a moment to breathe, talk and reset together. It's a small but powerful form of collective care woven into the workday, a reminder that restoration doesn't require permission – only intention.

In Japan, the practice of *Shinrin-yoku*, or 'forest bathing', offers another form of mindful renewal.[46] People slow down, walk among trees and reconnect with their senses – a simple ritual that reduces stress and restores focus.

It's not escape; it's recalibration – a reminder that care often begins with paying attention to what's already around us.

These examples show that self-care isn't always private, scheduled or loud. Sometimes it's a pattern in how we live together – simple rituals that keep the tide from taking too much at once.

Challenge the hypothesis

In this chapter, we've argued that caring for yourself is not a luxury but a leadership responsibility. Let's pause and ask: Is that actually true or is it just another modern comfort dressed up as wisdom?

The counterargument writes itself. History is full of leaders who delivered extraordinary results while ignoring their own limits. They slept little, worked endlessly and seemed to thrive on pressure. Discipline, not downtime, built empires. Why insist that self-care matters?

Because while endurance can carry you through a season, it rarely sustains a lifetime. What looks like strength in the moment often reveals itself as erosion over time. We've all seen it – the executive who outperforms until burnout ends the run, the team that crushes targets but loses half its people, the culture that confuses exhaustion for excellence.

Still, the scepticism is worth hearing. Maybe 'self-care' can slide into indulgence. Maybe it is easier for those with privilege, time or control over their calendars. Maybe boundaries can turn into walls. All of that is true – and it's why the definition must be sharper.

Self-care is not an escape from responsibility, it's the discipline that keeps responsibility possible.

It's not softness, it's stamina. It's not private, it's contagious.

Leaders who ignore their own renewal may win moments but they lose continuity, clarity and compassion. In the long run, that costs more than any day off ever will.

When care for yourself is missing

When care for self disappears, it rarely looks like neglect. It often looks like control.

Like the long-distance runner who trims every ounce of weight to go faster – and crosses the line thinner, quicker, weaker. For a while, it works. The body sharpens, the metrics rise, but the same discipline that once built strength slowly starts feeding on itself.

Leadership can follow the same pattern. We optimise every minute, perfect every process, curate every signal of success. To the outside world, it looks impressive – the constant motion, the calm tone, the flawless façade – but inside, energy runs on fumes. Presence becomes performance. The body, the mind and the spirit start borrowing from tomorrow to survive today.

Social media only amplifies the illusion. We share our best moments, our neat routines, our 'balance'. We perform resilience until we no longer have any left.

The absence of self-care rarely announces itself with a breakdown. It hides in small sacrifices – skipping rest, numbing fatigue, saying just one more week.

Because the early rewards are real – promotions, praise, results – we mistake the warning signs for momentum. What begins as mastery ends as depletion.

By the time the system fails, it's often the parts that can't be easily measured – joy, connection, presence – that are already gone.

That's the paradox of neglect: it often wears the face of success – until it doesn't.

Next horizon: From practice to presence

The future of self-care will be shaped by both technology and intention – and how well we separate the two.

We're already seeing the rise of virtual mindfulness, AI coaches and wearables that track everything from sleep quality to stress levels. Our watches nudge us to breathe. Our phones count our steps, our calories, even our calm.

It's impressive – and a little ironic. We've built a world so fast that we now need machines to remind us to slow down.

Today, even a simple question like 'How was your night?' often sends us glancing at a screen before we check in with ourselves. We're learning to quantify recovery instead of feeling it, and if we're not careful, our tools for well-being can quietly become our next form of dependence.

The next frontier isn't more data, it's discernment.

The risk is that self-care becomes another performance – optimised, measured, shared. If every breath is logged, every meditation gamified and every habit tracked for productivity, we lose the very thing we're trying to preserve: presence.

There's also reason for hope.

A new wave of leaders and organisations are shifting the conversation from wellness as an individual responsibility to well-being as a system design. We're seeing companies replace 'perks' with predictability, psychological safety and time as a resource. We're seeing leaders model pauses instead of preaching them.

Technology will keep evolving, but the real revolution will be cultural – when renewal becomes as measurable, respected and planned as output.

In the end, the future of self-care may not be virtual at all. It may simply be a return to attention – the courage to be fully here, before we hurry on.

Maybe the next upgrade isn't digital at all.

Summary

This chapter has been about self-care – not as a prescription, but as an invitation. Pause for a moment – not to analyse but to notice.

Reflection questions

- What signals does your body give you when you're running on empty? How often do you listen?
- When was the last time you felt truly rested – not just recovered enough to keep going?
- What stories do you tell yourself to justify exhaustion? Whose voice do they echo?
- How does the way you treat your own energy shape the tone of your team?
- If you suddenly stepped away tomorrow, what would your absence reveal – a system that sustains itself or one that depends on your overextension?
- Where in your week could renewal become a designed rhythm, not a stolen moment?
- What are you pretending not to notice about your own depletion?
- If presence really is the next upgrade, what might you need to uninstall first?

Leadership learnings

- Self-care is not indulgence – it's endurance made sustainable.
- Leaders who ignore their own renewal don't just burn themselves out; they quietly teach others that depletion is the price of belonging.

- Caring for yourself is not a withdrawal from responsibility but a preparation for it.
- Presence and perspective require energy – and energy requires design.
- True care grows in systems that make recovery legitimate, not heroic.
- When renewal is built into the rhythm of work, resilience becomes collective, not personal.
- In the end, leadership is less about how much you can give and more about how wisely you renew what you have to give again.

Ask from the author

There are very few truths in life that fit everyone.

For me, the way back from depletion came through movement and nutrition. For others, it might come through stillness, creativity, faith or time in nature.

There is no single doorway to renewal – only the one that opens from the inside.

I'm inspired by people like Dan Harris, who found his way through mindfulness and honesty. I'm equally moved by a close friend who once told me how stressful it felt when everyone around her was meditating and talking about awareness. 'It's just not for me,' she said – and I realised she was right.

Self-care that becomes comparison is just another form of pressure, so let's be careful when we talk about what helps us. Let's stay curious about what helps others.

Remember: the purpose of self-care isn't to become perfect – it's to stay present, to keep showing up, to keep the tide from taking too much at once.

Take care of yourself – not as a trend but as a truth – because you, and the people around you, truly need you whole.

INTERLUDE ONE

A LI'L ANTI FABLE: FROM COLONY TO CARE

The colony was a model of order.

Thousands of ants, perfectly aligned, marching in rhythm towards purpose. No distractions, no delays, no self-doubt. The hum of productivity filled every tunnel – a kind of underground heartbeat that pulsed with certainty.

In the middle of it all was Li'l Anti – small but fast, eager to contribute, eager to belong. He carried crumbs twice his size, never missed a turn and measured his worth by how quickly the pile grew.

The colony rewarded that. Efficiency was sacred. Reflection was waste.

Until one day, the Queen's council gathered and announced something new: 'We must care more.'

The tunnels buzzed. A new initiative. Banners went up: *'Care is productivity!'* Teams formed, charts were drawn, slogans echoed through the chambers.

Every ant was told to 'lead with care'. They nodded enthusiastically, though none were quite sure what that meant.

Li'l Anti tried his best. He smiled wider. He complimented more. He asked others if they were OK – mostly while running. Meetings became longer. Check-ins multiplied. Soon there were forms for feelings and metrics for empathy.

Care had become another task.

As the colony grew busier with its caring, something strange began to happen. The lines slowed. The crumbs piled unevenly. The tunnels, once alive with motion, filled with confusion.

Li'l Anti began to worry. He missed the rhythm. He missed the simplicity. He wondered whether care had made them weak.

That's when the Antocrat – one of the old guard – spoke loudly in the Great Chamber: 'We've gone soft! We need discipline, not dialogue. No more time wasted on feelings.'

A murmur of agreement spread through the crowd. Within hours, the banners were gone. The charts were replaced with quotas. The word 'care' was quietly buried under the weight of results.

For a while, the colony thrived again. The rhythm returned. The pile grew. But Li'l Anti noticed something different. The tunnels felt colder. The hum of work sharper, emptier.

He began to wonder whether both worlds – the caring chaos and the disciplined cold – were missing the same thing.

Late one night, he stayed behind, watching the lines of ants march past. He thought about all their efforts to add care – meetings, slogans, rules – and he realised that care had never needed to be added. It had only needed to be remembered.

The next day, Li'l Anti tried something different. He didn't talk about care; he practised it quietly. He noticed when another ant was struggling and helped without reporting it. He paused when carrying crumbs, making space for others to pass. He began to see that care wasn't a project, it was a way of being in the work.

The pile still grew, but so did something else – a kind of calm rhythm that spread through the tunnels, unseen but unmistakable. It wasn't slower, it was steadier.

For the first time, the hum of the colony didn't sound like work. It sounded like life.

Leadership commentary

This fable teaches us that care is not something leaders add to performance – it is the quality of attention that shapes how work is done, decisions are made and people are treated along the way.

Care factor connection

This opening interlude introduces the foundational paradox of *The Care Factor*: that care is often misunderstood as either softness or inefficiency, when in fact it is what makes performance human and sustainable. It sets the tone for the book's early chapters, where care is explored as a leadership stance rather than an initiative.

Leadership insight

The colony's initial response to care – turning it into banners, slogans and metrics – reflects a familiar leadership mistake. When care is treated as a programme, it becomes another task to optimise, measure and perform. In doing so, leaders unintentionally drain it of meaning.

The backlash that follows is equally instructive. When care becomes performative or bureaucratic, the instinctive reaction is often to swing back towards discipline, control and results at any cost. This false choice – care or performance – is at the heart of many leadership failures.

Li'l Anti's quiet realisation reframes the problem. Care does not need to be added to the work; it needs to be practised within it. It lives in small, often invisible decisions: noticing strain, making space, helping without reporting it. When care becomes a way of being rather than a declared priority, efficiency does not disappear – it steadies.

For leaders, the lesson is simple but demanding: stop announcing care and start embodying it. Care is not another layer of work, it is the rhythm beneath it.

Author reflection

Sometimes we mistake care for a performance – a new initiative, a better slogan, another layer of meetings – but real care doesn't live in programmes or policies. It lives in the spaces between them – in how we choose to move, listen and lift together.

Li'l Anti reminds us that care isn't what we add to the work, it's how we do the work. It doesn't make us less efficient, it makes our efficiency human.

Reflection for the reader

Ask yourself:

- Where in my leadership have I tried to add care instead of weaving it in?
- What would it look like if care became the rhythm beneath the results, not another measure of them?

4
Caring About Ethics And Values: The Compass

A compass always points north. For centuries, explorers relied on it to cross oceans and traverse uncharted territories. The compass didn't calm the waves, stop the storms or remove the dangers, but it offered orientation when everything else was shifting.

Its simplicity is also its strength. A compass is just a needle aligning with the earth's magnetic field, yet it never loses its truth. Maps, on the other hand, become outdated as borders shift, roads change or new lands are discovered. GPS devices offer speed and accuracy but depend on satellites, signals and batteries – all things that can fail at the worst possible time.

The compass never fails to point true north. That reliability is what made it indispensable to generations of travellers. It didn't give them the full picture, but it gave them enough to stay oriented.

Leadership is no different. Dashboards, AI models and quarterly scorecards are immensely useful, but they can be misleading, outdated or fragile. Values and ethics, however, are timeless. They don't guarantee smooth sailing, but they prevent drift. They keep leaders from losing their way when pressure, temptation or uncertainty clouds the view.

> **FUN FACT: The compass in history**
>
> The magnetic compass was invented in China during the Han dynasty, over 2,000 years ago, first for divination and later for navigation. It reached Europe by the 1100s and became the silent partner of explorers such as Columbus and Magellan. Without it, the Age of Discovery would have been impossible.[47]
>
> Tools change, but timeless orientation remains. Just as the compass unlocked new worlds, values unlock sustainable leadership.

Leadership in practice: The silent shortcut

This is far from my proudest moment – possibly the opposite – but I feel I have to share it.

Early in my career, I made a decision I still regret. During final negotiations with a client, I realised they had miscalculated assumptions in their financial model. Their error made our proposal look significantly cheaper than it actually was.

My mind raced. If I correct them, will they walk away? Will they turn the conversation against me? Am I trying to make them buy something they can't actually afford? Another voice whispered: They should have caught their own mistake. Maybe it's not my responsibility. Maybe staying silent is just smart business.

As anyone who has ever sat in a tense negotiation knows, the air itself can feel heavy. This one was no different. Every second stretched. Speaking up risked derailing everything. Staying silent felt easier, even justifiable.

I stayed silent and we won the contract. On the surface, it was a victory, but almost immediately, doubt crept in. I couldn't shake a gnawing guilt. Had I just crossed a line? What did it say about me if my success came through silence – through dishonesty?

That uneasy feeling followed me for weeks. When the error inevitably came to light, the damage cut even deeper. The client didn't just question the numbers; they questioned me. Our relationship never fully recovered. The business never became what either party had wanted or envisioned. What looked like a win in the moment left a scar – a reminder of the cost of compromise.

That experience has stayed with me ever since. I learnt that silence can be as loud as dishonesty. Today, even when it is uncomfortable, I choose transparency.

PARADOX ALERT: Transparency vs. protection

Speaking up risks the deal; staying silent protects the win. The very silence that feels like protection in the moment becomes the seed of mistrust later.

Leaders who choose transparency may lose the short-term prize – but they win the long-term relationship. Think of a leader who withholds bad news from employees to 'protect morale'. In the short term, it works – people remain calm – but when the truth surfaces, as it always does, morale collapses faster and deeper. Transparency may sting today but it builds trust for tomorrow.

Defining ethics, morals and values

Before diving further, it's important to pause and clarify what we mean by ethics, morals and values – terms often used interchangeably but that carry distinct weight.

Values are the deeply held beliefs that guide behaviour. They can differ across cultures, organisations and individuals. What one society prizes as loyalty, another may see as favouritism. Values are personal and contextual.

Morals describe the social norms and shared codes of conduct that define right and wrong in a given community. They are more collective than individual, shaping what groups accept or reject.

Ethics provides the framework to navigate dilemmas when values and morals collide. Ethics is not just about avoiding scandal – it is the compass leaders use to make decisions in grey zones, where no map exists.

For this book, when I share my stories, I do so from the lens of my own values and professional context. Different cultures, different readers, may calibrate differently. That is precisely why a compass matters: it gives orientation without pretending there is only one path.

Leadership in practice: The tender dilemma

When I was a general manager in a country organisation, one of our biggest customers was preparing for a new tender. They were about to issue a request for proposal, and when the documents came in they looked almost too good – polished, precise and suspiciously aligned with our capabilities. At first glance, it felt like fortune had smiled on us, but something gnawed at me.

I asked my head of sales for input on the process, and soon discovered that this account was managed by our star sales representative. After some digging, it came to light that this sales person was close friends with the customer's head of procurement. Together, they had written the tender documents – effectively designing the requirements so that only we could qualify.

On paper, it looked like a guaranteed win. In reality, it was a clear violation of both external laws and our company's internal ethics code. The dilemma was sharp: do we stay silent, pretend not to know and secure a massive deal – or do we step forward and risk losing everything?

The discussions inside our leadership team were long and painful. There was so much at stake. Yet the deeper questions kept returning: What would it say about us if we won through dishonesty? Would the short-term win be worth the long-term cost of trust? In the end, we made the hard choice: we disclosed the situation directly to the customer's head of operations.

The customer responded by halting the project for a year. Internally, we took the opportunity to train our sales force, ensuring they understood not only the rules but the spirit of ethical conduct. The sales person received a written warning and was removed from the account.

Here is the paradox: by admitting the issue and choosing transparency, our relationship with the customer grew stronger. A year later, when the tender was relaunched – this time clean and fair – we competed openly and still won. Not because the system had been bent but because we had earned trust in the right way.

That experience reminded me that care in leadership is not just about protecting numbers but about protecting integrity. Sometimes doing what seems most costly in the short run is what secures the deepest gains for the future.

FUN FACT: The origin of 'whistleblower'

The term 'whistleblower' comes from nineteenth-century British policemen who literally blew whistles to alert others of wrongdoing.[48] Over time, the word evolved into a symbol of those who raise the alarm when they see misconduct inside organisations.

Some of the most famous whistleblowers in history – Daniel Ellsberg (releasing the Pentagon Papers),[49] Sherron Watkins (giving internal warnings at Enron),[50] and Frances Haugen (exposing internal research regarding Facebook's impact on users and society)[51] – show how one voice can reveal truths entire systems try to hide.

Whistleblowers are often painted as troublemakers but they are really caretakers of integrity. Listening to them early can prevent crises later.

Corporate case stories

The corporate world offers a sobering map of what happens when leaders lose their compass – and what happens when they keep it.

Enron: From hero to zero

Enron was once hailed as a model of innovation. Behind the scenes, deception had become strategy. When the house of cards collapsed, employees lost pensions, investors lost billions and the very name 'Enron' became shorthand for corporate fraud.[52]

Wells Fargo: The scandal of the fake accounts

Wells Fargo pushed employees to open millions of fake accounts to meet aggressive sales targets.[53] The numbers looked stellar for a while, but when the fraud surfaced, the brand was shattered and leaders faced congressional hearings. Targets were hit but trust was destroyed.

Exxon Valdez: Another dimension of neglect

Cutting corners on safety led to one of the worst oil spills in history for Exxon Valdez.[54] The environmental and community damage lasted decades. A reminder that ethics isn't only about honesty – it's about responsibility.

Theranos: The ticking bomb in med tech

I followed the Theranos story[55] closely from my professional world in diagnostics and med tech. At first, it seemed like a miracle: revolutionary blood testing with just a drop of blood. Investors lined up, media celebrated, but inside, the technology didn't work.

Instead of admitting it, leaders doubled down on secrecy and spin. Patients were misled, doctors were misinformed, and when the truth came out, the crash was as dramatic as the rise. For me, watching Theranos was a professional and personal lesson: ambition without integrity is a ticking bomb.

Boeing 737 MAX: A very painful story

Under pressure to compete with Airbus, Boeing rushed development of the Boeing 737 MAX, compromised on safety and silenced internal warnings. Leadership decisions, cultural pressures and ethical failures contributed to the accidents and subsequent grounding of the aircraft. The crashes that followed killed hundreds and scarred one of the proudest names in aviation.[56] Once again, the compass had been lost.

Unilever: How to do things right

There are counterexamples. Paul Polman at Unilever refused to play the quarterly earnings game. He focused on long-term value creation and sustainability, even when analysts mocked him.[57] Over time, his compass – anchored in purpose – proved not only right but profitable. Unilever thrived, and Polman became a role model for how leaders can align values and performance.

The lesson

This teaches us that an ethical approach to results can prove to be the most long-term sustainable approach.

Insights from thinkers

Across these analyses, a consistent ethical lesson emerges: when commercial urgency eclipses core values, organisations begin to normalise small compromises that quietly erode safety, transparency and responsibility – until the system itself becomes dangerous. The Boeing 737 MAX case shows how decisions framed as technical or competitive were, at their heart, moral choices to prioritise speed over diligence, market positioning over human life and internal harmony over uncomfortable truth. A values-anchored organisation treats safety not as a constraint, but as a non-negotiable expression of care. They treat engineers, pilots and regulators as partners in stewardship rather than obstacles, and see speaking up as a duty, not a risk. The deeper learning is that ethics cannot be bolted on through compliance alone – they must be lived daily through leadership behaviour, incentives and culture. When values are clear and embodied, they function as a compass. When they are diluted, even brilliant organisations can lose their way.

Care is all around: Micro-acts guiding major change

Sometimes the clearest proof of values guiding direction isn't found in boardrooms or crisis meetings – it's in everyday life.

Transport for London once ran a campaign promoting kindness, civility and ethical behaviour in public transport environments by urging passengers to notice 'small acts of kindness': a stranger giving up a seat, someone holding a door, a fellow commuter helping with heavy bags.[58] None of these gestures sped up the train, but they changed how people felt about the journey. Care made the system more human, even though the timetable remained the same.

The same lesson shows up in unexpected corners of corporate life. Nordstrom, the US retailer famous for its service culture, has long empowered employees to 'do the right thing' for customers, even if it means breaking a rule.[59] The company's unofficial stories – like an employee reportedly accepting a customer's return of snow tyres, despite the fact Nordstrom doesn't sell tyres – may be embellished over time, but they symbolise something important: small acts of dignity and respect define culture more than any poster on the wall.

Cultural traditions carry the same message. In Japan, the bow is more than a polite greeting – it is a micro-gesture of respect, an acknowledgement of the other person's dignity. No transaction is too small for this moment of recognition. The bow is not just etiquette; it is an ethical signal that says: you matter.

When leaders pay attention to these micro-moments, they realise something powerful: ethics is not only about grand dilemmas but about respect in the everyday. How people are spoken to in meetings, how credit is shared, whether kindness is offered when no one is watching – these choices create the real compass of culture.

Compliance and ethics officers belong here too. They rarely make headlines, but they quietly shape whether these small acts of honesty or dishonesty are tolerated. They are the keepers of everyday integrity, often invisible until something goes wrong. Seen in the right light, they are not bureaucrats slowing things down – they are caregivers of trust, ensuring that the little things align with the big principles.

In this way, care really is all around. It's often in those smallest choices – holding a door, accepting a return, bowing in respect or enforcing a rule gently but firmly – that an organisation's true compass becomes visible.

Challenge the hypothesis

If ethics and values are a leader's compass, does that mean they always lead to good outcomes? Not necessarily.

History offers sobering reminders that a compass can be steady – and still point the wrong way. Loyalty, for example, can be celebrated as a strength, but when taken too far it can become cover for wrongdoing. Efficiency may drive innovation, but when prized above all else, it can justify sacrificing people in pursuit of output. Even noble values can mutate into blind spots when applied without reflection.

One of the most insidious risks is groupthink – when shared values like harmony, loyalty or alignment are over-applied. In corporate life, this often shows up as a subtle silencing of dissent.[60] Leaders say they welcome challenge, but their behaviour makes people hesitant to speak up. Meetings become echo chambers where consensus is prized more than truth. The result? Bad decisions are rubber-stamped because no one dares to ask the uncomfortable question.

History is full of cautionary tales. The Challenger space shuttle disaster in 1986 is one: engineers raised concerns about faulty O-rings in cold weather, but leadership, under pressure to launch, suppressed the warnings. The collective value of 'staying on schedule' outweighed the ethical obligation to pause. The cost was catastrophic.[61]

Another danger is not a single big decision but the slow creep of many small ones. In Sweden, a series of scandals emerged when local politicians were found to have used taxpayers' money for expensive trips and fine dining. What started as something seemingly minor – approving a beer at Friday lunch – escalated into normalised abuse of funds. Each step felt small, but over time the slope grew steep.

The same is true in business. A slight bending of reporting rules, a 'temporary' adjustment to meet quarterly targets, a white lie told to protect the brand – each small compromise lays groundwork for a culture where much bigger compromises become thinkable. By the time the organisation realises how far it has drifted, the compass is no longer pointing north.

There is also the complexity of cultural differences. Values that feel natural in one country can feel questionable in another. Gift-giving, for example, may be seen as respect in some cultures and bribery in others. A leader who insists their own cultural compass is 'the only true north' risks miscalibration in global contexts. Here the ethical challenge is not about abandoning values but about learning to navigate multiple compasses without losing integrity.

These examples remind us that values and ethics are not static; they must be stress-tested, questioned and recalibrated. A compass is only useful if it's aligned with true north – dignity, integrity and care. Otherwise, leaders may feel oriented but still lead their people astray.

The challenge, then, is not just to carry a compass but to keep checking: Is it calibrated? Is it aligned with what really matters? Without that discipline, even the most value-driven leader can drift into dangerous waters.

In the end, the real danger is not being without a compass – it is assuming that the one you hold is automatically correct. Leadership demands vigilance: to test, recalibrate and sometimes even challenge the values we hold most dear. The true strength of an ethical compass is not just in pointing north but in reminding us to keep asking if the direction we are heading in is still worth following.

When the compass is missing

Not everyone carries a compass. Research shows that a small percentage of leaders may exhibit traits of psychopathy or sociopathy – personality structures marked by lack of empathy, disregard for rules and manipulation for personal gain.[62] These individuals can be highly charismatic, persuasive and successful in the short term – often rising quickly because they project certainty and charm. Yet beneath the surface, their absence of care creates toxic cultures, broken trust and long-term damage.

The danger is subtle: because they are often excellent performers and storytellers, organisations may celebrate them until the consequences surface. History is full of corporate scandals fuelled not just by bad decisions but by leaders whose compass never existed in the first place.

For the rest of us, this is a sobering reminder: not every confident leader deserves to be followed. Part of caring leadership is learning to recognise when someone is steering without a compass – and protecting both people and organisations from the fallout.

Next horizon: Ethical leadership in practice

There's an eternal pattern: technology advances faster than our ability to regulate or ethically navigate it. Yesterday, it was industrialisation, nuclear energy and genetic engineering. Today, it is AI, deepfakes and biotechnology. Tomorrow, it will be something new.

The danger is always the same: leaders who only trust their 'maps' – dashboards, forecasts, algorithms – risk drift when the storm comes. Leaders who carry a compass – values, integrity, care – can adapt because they remain oriented when everything else shifts.

Ethics doesn't stop at national borders. As organisations become more global, leaders face dilemmas shaped by culture, regulation and inequality. What is considered acceptable in one country might be seen as corruption in another. Labour standards, environmental practices and human rights are constantly tested by the tension between local norms and universal values.

Even pandemics revealed how fragile our ethical frameworks can be. Nations hoarded vaccines, supply chains buckled and national interests often trumped global solidarity. The next crisis may well test whether we have learnt to align care with cooperation.

Another horizon challenge is trust itself. In polarised societies, even facts are contested. Leaders today operate in an environment where disinformation spreads faster than truth and transparency is both more demanded and distrusted than ever.

As the world grows more interconnected, the foundations of trust grow more fragile. Ethical leadership in this context isn't about finding perfect solutions – it's about modelling integrity so consistently that trust can be rebuilt, piece by piece.

Imagine this: your company develops an AI tool that can diagnose a serious disease earlier and more accurately than any human doctor. The catch? The treatment it identifies costs hundreds of thousands of dollars per patient. Your algorithm can save lives, but mostly for the wealthy. The data shows that in poorer regions, patients will get the diagnosis – and then be left without options. Investors want to scale the product quickly. Doctors are divided. Regulators are watching closely.

What would you do? This is not just a business question – it is a compass question. Do you prioritise innovation, access, profit or fairness? There is no easy answer, but how you choose will define whether your compass holds steady in the storm.

Summary

Take some time to think about your own compass and ponder what you have learnt from this chapter.

Reflection questions

- Can you think of a situation where staying silent felt easier than speaking up? What choice did you make?
- Did you ever notice a small compromise growing into something larger over time? How did it unfold?
- Have you experienced a clash between cultural norms and your own ethical compass? How did you navigate it?
- When was the last time you questioned whether your compass was still calibrated to what truly matters?
- If a whistleblower came to you tomorrow, how would you respond – with defensiveness or with care?

Leadership learnings

- A clear compass doesn't prevent storms, but it prevents drift.
- Shortcuts may win contracts but destroy trust.
- Betrayal tempts retaliation but resilience strengthens integrity.
- Compliance is not bureaucracy – it is care for culture.
- Values, when lived daily, become the shield against scope creep.
- Leaders must keep recalibrating their compass – without this discipline, even good intentions can go astray.

Ask from the author

One of the hardest truths I've learnt is that ethical drift rarely happens in one dramatic leap. It happens in tiny steps. A small compromise here, a 'just this once' exception there – until suddenly, you find yourself standing in a place that, a few years earlier, you would have judged as completely unacceptable.

I still carry the scar from a client meeting early in my career, where I chose silence over transparency. At the time, it felt like nothing more than letting an error pass, but the consequences were lasting. A relationship never fully recovered, and I was left with a permanent reminder that small compromises leave deep marks.

The same creep shows up in public life. Remember the Swedish scandal, where local politicians ended up exposed for expensive trips and fine dinners at taxpayers' expense. This didn't begin with a five-star hotel; it began with something small – someone ordering a beer at a Friday lunch. One step led to another, and before long, the line between public duty and private indulgence was erased.

My ask to you is simple: keep your compass at hand. Don't delegate ethics to a department or a compliance officer. Make it part of your own daily decision-making, as natural as reviewing a budget or approving a strategy.

The storms of business will always tempt you to trade a little integrity for a little progress, but every 'little' trade leaves a mark. The leaders who stand out are those who refuse to let small compromises accumulate into big regrets.

5

Caring About Innovation: Bringing The Blocks Together

At first glance, a Lego brick is simple – a small, colourful piece of plastic with no obvious purpose on its own. The genius of Lego is not in the individual brick; it's in the infinite combinations. A single block may look ordinary, but connect it with others and suddenly you can build a house, a bridge, a spaceship – limited only by imagination.

Innovation works in the same way. Rarely does a breakthrough come from one isolated idea. It comes from connecting, recombining and reimagining what already exists. Think of the smartphone: not a brand-new invention but a combination of existing technologies – phone, camera, internet, music player – clicked together into something revolutionary.

Lego sets often come with detailed instructions to build a castle, a race car or a Star Wars spaceship. When you follow the manual, you get a predictable result – impressive, but the same as everyone else who bought that set. True creativity emerges when builders ignore the manual, mix pieces from different sets and invent something entirely their own.

Organisations face the same choice. They can push teams to execute according to rigid plans and KPIs – the predefined 'castle'. Or they can create room for experimentation, where people take risks, combine unlikely ideas and discover new solutions – the open play. The first produces efficiency; the second produces breakthroughs.

The Lego brick teaches us that innovation doesn't demand starting from scratch. It demands curiosity, courage to combine and a culture that allows people to see possibility where others see only plastic bricks.

Leadership in practice: Shifting the culture

I was still relatively new in my role as leader of a senior leadership team. They were used to working in a very specific way: professional, precise and clinical. The norm was simple – deliver on your KPI, finish your project, move on to the next. Success was defined by outcomes, not by how people got there.

At first, it seemed to work. Targets were being met, deliverables were produced on time. On paper, it was the picture of efficiency, but as the months went on, cracks began to show. Deadlines slipped more often. Tension rose in meetings. Instead of energy, I started to feel fatigue. People were delivering, but they weren't thriving.

I asked myself: Do I just push harder on the numbers or do I try something different?

The instinctive answer in a KPI-driven culture is always 'drive harder', but as results began to slip, it became clear to me that the solution was not more pressure on individuals, it was to rethink how we worked together.

We began to experiment. We set up small cross-functional hackathons where people could step outside their silos and solve problems creatively. We allowed employees to take 'innovation days' to work on ideas they were passionate about. We piloted job shadowing so team members could see challenges from another perspective. Not everything worked. Some ideas fizzled out quickly, others needed refinement, but something started to shift.

I remember when a group came back from a hackathon with an idea for automating part of a manual reporting process. It wasn't glamorous, but it saved hours of work every week. More importantly, the energy in the room was different. People were proud, not because they hit a KPI but because they created something together.

That was the spark. More small ideas followed: tweaks to workflows, new ways of sharing insights, practical process improvements. Bit by bit, the culture changed. Collaboration replaced isolation. Curiosity replaced defensiveness. The team still delivered results, but now they did it with a sense of ownership and creativity.

Almost like magic, the real breakthrough happened. Innovation didn't need to be commanded; it started to emerge naturally. People began to come forward with ideas before being asked. Teams started to self-organise to tackle problems. What had once been a culture of compliance was becoming a culture of care – where people weren't just working for their KPIs but with each other.

Looking back, I realise how fragile that shift was. If I had chosen the easy path of pushing harder on the numbers, the cracks would have deepened. By creating space to experiment – to try, to fail and to learn – we discovered a new way of working: one where care and collaboration unlocked more than pressure ever could.

PARADOX ALERT: Vulnerability vs. strength

In leadership, vulnerability is often mistaken for weakness. Yet in reality, it is one of the greatest sources of strength. Teams that never admit uncertainty may appear confident, but they miss the chance to learn. Leaders who pretend to have all the answers may look strong in the moment, but they prevent growth. When leaders create space for openness – admitting blind spots, inviting critique and showing they don't know it all – resilience and innovation multiply. Vulnerability does not diminish authority; it deepens trust and accelerates progress.

Leadership in practice: Innovating the business review

It's well known in business that reviews can be painful. There's a lot of preparation and the questions can be tough, sometimes even brutal. They can also reveal blind spots, force clarity and serve as a catalyst to improve both thinking and processes.

At one stage of my career, my team and I had been left out of the usual review cycle. We were performing well, and I suppose leadership's focus was elsewhere. When I told my team that I wanted us to pilot a new kind of business review, the looks I got were sceptical, to say the least. Instead of being relieved at our 'escape', here I was, inviting the scrutiny back in – and making it even more intense.

My idea was to run a peer review. We would invite a panel drawn from across the organisation – different levels, different functions – to go through our business in detail. Then, instead of ending with a one-way report, we would host a collaborative 'hack session' with senior leadership to generate insights and ideas.

To guide us, I drew on a concept from psychology called the Johari window. It's a simple but powerful framework that describes four quadrants of self-knowledge: what we see and others see (the open area), what we know but hide (the hidden area), what others see but we don't (the blind spot) and what no one yet sees (the unknown). My intent was to use this framework to shift the review away from the obvious metrics and instead focus on what was hidden or blind – the things that truly limited our growth.

As we prepared for the two-day session, I could see the team slowly warming to the idea. When the review came, something remarkable happened. The peer reviewers didn't just critique us; they invested their perspectives and creativity to help us. They surfaced blind spots we had never noticed and challenged assumptions we didn't realise we were carrying. The conversations were open, honest and constructive.

The impact went beyond the review itself. My boss and other senior leaders were impressed by the openness and courage of the team. They saw us not just as operators but as innovators. Inside the team, there was a new sense of pride: we had shown up fully, allowed ourselves to be vulnerable, and in doing so, discovered strength.

The lesson stayed with me: you can innovate anywhere, even in a business review. Sometimes the biggest breakthroughs come not from defending your performance but from inviting others in to challenge it.

FUN FACT: The origin of 'innovation'

The term innovation comes from the Latin *innovare*, meaning 'to renew or to make new', reflecting innovation as purposeful renewal rather than novelty for its own sake.[63] In medieval times it was often used with suspicion, associated with disruption and even heresy – innovators were people who challenged the established order. Today, the word carries a far more positive glow, but the essence remains: true innovation always challenges the status quo.

Defining innovation

Before exploring stories, paradoxes and lessons, it helps to pause and clarify what we mean by innovation. The word is everywhere – in boardrooms, annual reports and keynote speeches – but often it means very different things depending on who says it.

Invention is about creating something entirely new – a fresh technology, an original idea, a breakthrough that didn't exist before.

Improvement is about making something better – streamlining a process, enhancing a product or tweaking a service.

Innovation sits in the middle. It is the bridge between creativity and impact. An idea is not innovation until it is put into practice and creates value for people.

Innovation can be radical – changing the rules of the game – or incremental, improving the way we already play. Both matter. A new digital platform that transforms an industry and a small automation that saves employees hours each week are equally acts of innovation because they change outcomes.

Importantly, innovation is not limited to products or technologies. It can be cultural (how teams collaborate), organisational (how decisions are made) or social (how we serve communities). For commercial organisations, business model innovation is especially powerful: changing how value is created, delivered or captured can disrupt markets more than any single product.

For this book, when I talk about innovation, I mean the act of turning care and creativity into solutions that actually work and have impact. Not just clever ideas on sticky notes but actions that move people, teams or societies forward.

Innovation is not a department or a workshop – it is a mindset. When guided by care, it becomes less about chasing novelty and more about creating meaningful, sustainable impact. Innovation often begins with accidents – but it only changes the world when discipline shapes it into something useful.

FUN FACT: CRISPR – A serendipitous breakthrough

One of the most transformative tools in modern science, CRISPR gene editing was discovered not through a grand plan but by studying how bacteria fight viruses.[64] What seemed like a curiosity became a revolution, enabling precise DNA editing. The spark was serendipity, but only years of disciplined science turned it into a breakthrough that is reshaping medicine and agriculture.

Corporate case stories

Innovation is often spoken about as a technological race. But at its core, the most meaningful innovations begin with a values-driven question: Who are we here to serve, and what problem truly deserves our attention? The following cases show how ethics, care and courage can become powerful engines of innovation.

Médecins Sans Frontières (MSF): Frugal innovation in crisis

When bombs fall or floods sweep through, there is no luxury of perfect infrastructure. MSF teams have had to invent portable, resilient solutions: backpack-sized surgical kits, low-cost diagnostic tools, even inflatable hospitals that can be set up in a matter of hours.[65] These were not designed in high-tech labs but in the mud and dust of emergencies. The lesson is clear: innovation doesn't always mean cutting-edge technology – sometimes it's the ability to deliver care with almost nothing.

Grameen Bank: Banking on the poor

Muhammad Yunus saw something traditional banks could not: poor women in rural Bangladesh were not bad risks, they were the best credit partners. By offering small loans without collateral, Grameen created a model that transformed communities – and inspired microfinance worldwide.[66]

The repayment rates were higher than most commercial banks. The innovation was not a product but a business model, redefining who counted as a customer.

DARPA: Betting on the unknown

Out of fear of falling behind in the space race, the US government created the Advanced Research Projects Agency (ARPA, later DARPA – Defense Advanced Research Projects Agency) to fund bold, untested research. There were no guarantees and many projects failed. The ones that succeeded changed the world: the Internet, GPS and voice recognition.[67] The real innovation wasn't any single invention – it was the systematic willingness to fund uncertainty.

Tata Motors: The Nano car paradox

The Tata Nano was designed to bring safe, affordable mobility to millions of Indian families. On paper, it was brilliant: an engineering feat that delivered a working car at a fraction of the normal cost, but the marketing framed it as 'the world's cheapest car'.[68] Customers rejected it – no one wanted to drive a badge of poverty. The Nano became a cautionary tale: innovation must succeed not just technically but emotionally.

The Gates Foundation: Grand challenges

Some problems are too big for markets to solve alone. The Gates Foundation took a venture capital approach to global health: funding bold ideas like malaria vaccines, toilets that don't need sewage or crops engineered to withstand drought.[69] Many ideas fail, but some transform entire fields. Sometimes the greatest breakthroughs come from aiming at the challenges no one else wants to touch.

The lesson

From MSF we learn that constraint can be the mother of invention. Grameen Bank shows us that innovation isn't only what you build, it's who you choose to serve. DARPA proves that if leaders want breakthrough innovation, they must create space for risk, tolerate failure and think in decades, not quarters. Tata Motors goes to show that people don't buy just products – they buy meanings. The Gates Foundation embodies that innovation requires not only creativity but the courage to tackle the problems that others avoid.

Together, these cases remind us that innovation is not the privilege of tech hubs or billion-dollar budgets. It can emerge in refugee camps, rural villages, government labs or philanthropic experiments. Wherever leaders are willing to combine courage, creativity and care, innovation thrives – not just for profit but for people.

Insights from thinkers

The cases illustrate innovation in action. The thinkers below reveal the mindset behind it: a way of leading that treats innovation not as a race for novelty, but as an expression of care.

- **Clayton Christensen: Disruptive innovation** – In *The Innovator's Dilemma,* Clayton introduced the world to the idea of disruptive innovation.[70] His warning was clear: companies that only listen to their best customers and perfect their current offerings risk missing the smaller, cheaper, initially 'worse' innovations that later reshape entire industries. Think of how Netflix disrupted Blockbuster, or how smartphones devoured the market for cameras and MP3 players. Christensen's point is that true innovation often looks unimpressive at first – but it carries care for unmet needs that incumbents dismiss. Leaders who cultivate curiosity for these 'weak signals' show care not just for their current customers, but for the future ones they don't yet serve.

- **Peter Drucker: Innovation as discipline –** Peter, the father of modern management, saw innovation less as a stroke of genius and more as disciplined practice. He argued that leaders shouldn't wait for inspiration but instead search systematically: changes in demographics, shifts in consumer behaviour or new scientific knowledge all create fertile ground for innovation.

  For Drucker, innovation was not luck; it was responsibility. Care, in his framing, meant taking seriously the duty to look ahead, to notice shifts and to prepare organisations to meet them. A leader who fails to innovate, Drucker said, is neglecting the care of both employees and customers.[71]

- **Mariana Mazzucato: Innovation as a shared endeavour –** Mariana, an economist, flips the usual narrative by showing that many of the greatest innovations – from the internet to GPS to modern vaccines – were seeded not by lone geniuses in garages but by public investment and collective risk-taking. Her work challenges leaders to see innovation not as a private trophy but as a shared endeavour. For her, care is about building systems where public good and private enterprise reinforce each other. Ignoring that interdependence, she argues, undermines society's ability to tackle big challenges like climate change or inequality.[72]

- **IDEO: Solving people, not problems –** The design firm behind icons, such as Apple's first computer mouse, brought design thinking into the mainstream. Tim Brown and David Kelley popularised a human-centred approach: start not with technology or profit targets but with empathy.[73] Go out into the field; observe how people live, where they struggle, what delights them. From this posture of care, the most transformative ideas emerge – not because they are technically brilliant, but because they resonate deeply with human needs. Design thinking reframed innovation as not just problem-solving but *people*-solving.

Together, these thinkers remind us that innovation is not a single act but a spectrum: disruptive outsiders spotting overlooked needs, disciplined managers systematising the search, public institutions carrying shared risks and designers putting human dignity at the core. At its best, innovation is not just about novelty, it is about care in action.

Care is all around: Innovation in everyday life

When people hear the word 'innovation', they often picture labs filled with scientists, Silicon Valley start-ups or billion-dollar patents. Innovation doesn't just live in boardrooms or R&D departments, sometimes it's found in the smallest acts of care.

On the London Underground, station staff once introduced a simple 'priority seat' sign to encourage passengers to give up their spot for those who needed it.[74] Hardly cutting-edge technology, but the design was clever – it used warm colours and friendly illustrations rather than authoritarian language. A micro-innovation in signage transformed behaviour across the system. That is innovation too: seeing a human problem and solving it with empathy.

In Japanese convenience stores, customers can buy 'half portions' of prepared meals.[75] It sounds trivial, but it's an elegant response to two issues at once: reducing food waste and supporting elderly customers who may not need large portions. A small design tweak created value for both people and planet.

Corporate examples show the same spirit. As mentioned in Chapter 1, at 3M, the Post-It note wasn't born from a billion-dollar project but from a scientist's 'failed' experiment with a weak adhesive. Instead of shelving the mistake, he reframed it, thinking an adhesive that sticks lightly could be useful.[76] Care showed up in the willingness to protect a small idea that didn't fit the mould and the result became one of the world's most iconic office tools.

Even compliance and governance have their part in this story. Innovation doesn't always mean breaking rules; sometimes it's about creating space within them. When companies design 'sandboxes' – limited areas where teams can test new solutions without risking the whole system – they're practising care. They are protecting people and organisations from harm while still encouraging creativity.

Innovation is not just about moonshots. It's about noticing the small cracks where life could be easier, fairer or more humane – and doing something about it. Care and innovation are closer than most leaders think.

Challenge the hypothesis

If innovation is the lifeblood of organisations, does that mean more innovation is always better? Not necessarily.

There's a seductive myth in business today: the very act of innovating is inherently good. Leaders chase the next big thing, launching new features, products or campaigns just to show movement. Start-ups pitch themselves as 'disruptive' without asking what, exactly, they are disrupting – or whether it should be disrupted at all. Established companies pour resources into 'innovation labs' that generate prototypes for headlines, not for impact.

The danger is that innovation becomes an end in itself, detached from purpose or care. Shiny newness replaces meaningful progress. Think of consumer technology that updates so fast that devices are obsolete within months, fuelling mountains of e-waste, or food delivery apps that scale at breakneck speed without considering the rights of the workers who make the service possible. These aren't failures of creativity; they're failures of care.

History provides its warnings. In the early 2000s, Segway promised to revolutionise urban transport.[77] It was technically brilliant but blind to human behaviour: people didn't want to redesign cities around scooters that cost thousands of dollars. The result was innovation without impact – a reminder that novelty without need is just noise.

Contrast that with examples where care guided innovation. During the COVID-19 pandemic, companies that rapidly repurposed supply chains to produce ventilators or protective equipment didn't just innovate; they responded with care for lives. Their compass wasn't disruption for its own sake but service to people in need.

The lesson is clear: innovation alone is not the compass, care is. Innovation provides direction and energy, but care ensures it is calibrated towards dignity, responsibility and long-term value. Without care, innovation can drift into gimmickry or harm. With care, it becomes a force for progress that actually matters.

What does it all mean? The challenge is not simply to innovate, but to ask: Why are we innovating, who does it serve and what impact will it leave? Innovation without care risks becoming noise in a world already full of it. Innovation with care becomes a signal – a force that creates trust, strengthens communities and leaves behind solutions that endure. The true test of innovation is not how new it is but how deeply it matters.

When innovation is missing

I've seen firsthand how dangerous it can be when innovation is absent. On the surface, things look calm – targets are met, processes are followed, the machine keeps running – but underneath, you feel the energy fading. People stop suggesting improvements. Meetings become predictable. The organisation quietly drifts into irrelevance.

I remember sitting in a leadership meeting where someone raised the idea of digitising a key process. It wasn't radical, just common sense, but the response was: 'Let's not disturb what's already working.' The idea died right there – not because it was wrong, but because the culture was too comfortable. That moment stayed with me. It wasn't neglecting a big bet; it was neglecting the small signals that the world was moving on.

History is full of similar stories. Kodak invented the digital camera but shelved it to protect film sales.[78] Blockbuster dismissed Netflix, convinced that stores and late fees would always win.[79] Both companies were masters of their craft – until their refusal to innovate turned mastery into fragility.

Innovation missing isn't neutral. It's not 'steady' or 'safe'. It's a slow erosion of relevance. For people, it means feeling stuck. For organisations, it means being overtaken. For society, it means losing the progress that care and creativity could have delivered.

Next horizon: Innovation or manipulation?

Some of the most powerful innovations emerge not from abundance, but from scarcity. In Africa, India and parts of Latin America, frugal innovation has produced solutions like solar-powered medical devices, mobile banking systems and low-cost diagnostics that reach millions. These are reminders that innovation is not always about high-tech – it's about care expressed through ingenuity. When resources are limited, the best leaders find creative ways to solve real human problems with what is available.

Not all innovation is progress. In recent years, we've seen a rise in what might be called 'artificial innovation' – efforts that look new but serve more to distract or disguise than to improve. Greenwashing, sportswashing and other practices exploit the glow of 'innovation' to polish reputations while real issues remain unaddressed. For example, corporations may launch a flashy sustainability campaign while quietly expanding harmful practices elsewhere. Governments may sponsor high-tech spectacles while ignoring systemic problems. These are innovations in image, not in substance. They remind us that innovation without care risks becoming manipulation.

Imagine your company develops a revolutionary material that can dramatically cut carbon emissions in construction. The catch? It requires a rare mineral sourced from politically unstable regions, raising concerns about exploitation and conflict. Investors want to scale production quickly, environmental groups are watching, regulators are divided. What would you do?

This is not just a technical or financial question – it is a compass question. Do you prioritise environmental gain at the cost of social harm? Do you wait for a cleaner solution and risk losing momentum? Do you innovate further to find an alternative? How leaders navigate these dilemmas will define not just their strategy, but their legacy.

Summary

Take a moment to pause and think about the knowledge and insights you have gained in this chapter.

Reflection questions

- Can you recall a moment when innovation felt alive – when an idea energised people far beyond its size?
- Did you ever witness a simple act of curiosity that opened the door to something bigger than anyone expected?
- What would happen if you treated every half-formed idea as a seed – not to be judged but to be nurtured?
- Where in your team or organisation might quiet innovators already be at work, waiting to be seen and supported?
- If innovation is both gift and responsibility, how do you make sure it builds a future worth caring about?

Leadership learnings

- Innovation is not luck – it is a discipline of curiosity, courage and care.

- Small experiments often spark the biggest shifts. Create space for them.
- Vulnerability is not weakness. It can be the catalyst for collaboration and resilience.
- Innovation without purpose risks becoming noise. Anchor it in impact.
- The best leaders don't demand creativity – they design environments where it can flourish.

Ask from the author

Innovation is a force too powerful to leave to chance. It is not about chasing every shiny idea or forcing creativity on demand. It is about channelling energy – much like a Formula 1 driver unleashes the full power of the car but only by steering with precision and care.

My ask to you is this: make space for innovation, but never lose sight of purpose. Nurture curiosity, protect experiments and celebrate progress – but always ask, to what end? Innovation that does not serve people, the planet or long-term trust is not innovation – it is distraction.

As you lead, carry this balance: bold enough to experiment, careful enough to channel and wise enough to ensure that what you create is truly worth building.

6

Caring About Diversity: The Spice That Brings It All Together

Diversity is like cooking a great meal. Each ingredient brings its own flavour, texture and character. Some are strong and spicy, others subtle and grounding. Alone, they can be nourishing, but when combined thoughtfully they create something richer, more complex and far more satisfying.

Think of cuisines around the world: Indian curries layering spice upon spice, Italian dishes balancing acidity and sweetness, Japanese cooking highlighting umami. What makes them memorable is not one dominant flavour but the harmony of differences.

Organisations are no different. If everyone thinks the same way, it's like cooking with only salt. You may get something edible, but it won't surprise or delight. True innovation and resilience come from blending different perspectives, experiences and skills – even when the process is messy or the flavours clash at first.

Just as cuisines spread and mix across cultures – think of sushi burritos or Korean tacos – workplaces thrive when ideas and practices travel, evolve and fuse into something new. Diversity doesn't just add variety; it sparks creativity and growth.

I, for one, could not imagine a life without chillis – a little spice goes a long way.

FUN FACT: Chilli around the world

Did you know that chilli peppers are among the most widely grown crops on earth? More than 40 million tonnes are produced every year, across nearly every continent.[80] Chilli has travelled far from its origins in Central and South America to become a truly global spice. In Mexico you find smoky chipotles, in India the fiery bhut jolokia and in southern Europe the milder peppers that give depth rather than heat.

Chilli shows how diversity creates richness: one plant, adapted into thousands of varieties, each bringing its own intensity and character. Just as cuisines around the world thrive by combining flavours, diverse perspectives in teams add spice and depth that no single ingredient could deliver alone.

Leadership in practice: Pulled apart in California

It was an early morning in September, the California sun already warm as I walked into the conference room. I was 30 years old, proud of what I had achieved in the Nordics and eager to prove myself on a bigger stage. The team was diverse in every sense – different nationalities, industries and ways of working. For me, this was a chance to stretch my wings.

The meeting started well. I delivered my presentation with the same confidence that had carried me through countless boardrooms back home, but almost immediately, the questions came. Sharp, probing, relentless. Instead of nods of approval, I was met with scepticism. What I thought were solid arguments were picked apart, line by line.

At first, I tried to hold steady, but soon I felt pulled apart – my confidence slipping with each new challenge. A wave of self-doubt rose inside me. Why didn't they see the logic? Why were they attacking me? Underneath the professional composure, I felt anger flicker. For the first time in years, I wasn't sure I belonged at the table.

In that discomfort, something shifted. I realised the problem wasn't only with them – it was with me. I had come in with assumptions, blind spots shaped by a culture where harmony and consensus were prized. Here, the culture rewarded direct challenge, sharp debate and intellectual sparring. What felt like an attack was, in fact, their way of showing engagement.

The weeks that followed were a crash course in humility. Working day by day with this truly diverse team, I started to see how many of my own hidden biases had shaped me – assumptions I hadn't even known I had carried. Slowly, I became less defensive and more curious. I listened harder. I asked more questions. I grew, not only as a leader but as a person.

Looking back, that morning in California was a gift wrapped in discomfort. It forced me to confront myself, to unlearn and to rebuild. Diversity wasn't just a concept anymore; it became the crucible in which my leadership was tested and transformed.

PARADOX ALERT: Comfort vs. challenge

Diversity feels easy when it's about representation, celebration or harmony, but its true value often emerges in discomfort – when ideas clash, assumptions are questioned and leaders are forced to confront perspectives that unsettle them. What first feels like friction can actually become the spark for stronger solutions.

Psychologist Charlan Nemeth, in her research on dissent, found that even when 'dissenters' are wrong, their presence improves group creativity, decision quality and critical thinking.[81] Why? Because they force others to step back, examine assumptions and search for alternatives they might otherwise overlook. In the same way, diversity pushes us beyond easy consensus. Without that challenge, it risks becoming decoration – pleasant but powerless.

If the first story taught me how diversity can challenge the individual, this next one showed me how diversity – especially when it collides with comfort – can transform an entire idea.

Leadership in practice: The flight that changed the project

We had just wrapped up a boot-camp style offsite. The goal: to design a new business model that could bring patients and physicians closer in managing a chronic condition. The team was diverse in function – business, engineering, legal – but culturally we were similar: all Western Europeans. That sameness felt easy. We built rapport quickly, agreed on an idea and worked intensely for days to polish it. When we left, we were proud of what we had built.

The next day, I boarded a long transatlantic flight with a female colleague from a different cultural background. During the flight, I shared our idea. To my surprise, she reacted strongly – even emotionally. She found the entire concept repulsive, intrusive. I grew defensive. Surely she had misunderstood. I explained again, but the more I spoke, the more upset she became. We spent nearly the whole flight in tense argument, not rest.

The following day, still tired from the journey, we had to work side by side. Something shifted. I noticed how she approached questions differently to the way I did, and I became curious. At the end of the day, I asked for a meeting to dig deeper into her perspective. This time, instead of defending, I listened. Suddenly her points made sense. Her cultural lens exposed ethical and emotional dimensions we had completely missed.

We began co-creating, not by compromising but by leaning into the tension between our views. A new, stronger concept emerged. When I brought it back to the team, I had to convince them to embrace the changes. To my relief, the colleague herself stepped up as a sponsor of the idea. Together, we built something far more robust than our original version.

PARADOX ALERT: Embracing tension to unlock innovation

Teams that only value harmony risk mediocrity. It is in the clash of perspectives – the friction that feels uncomfortable – that real innovation often emerges. Leaders who dare to invite, hold and channel that tension don't just build better ideas; they build stronger teams.

Defining diversity, equity and inclusion

Diversity is often misunderstood as a numbers game – how many women, how many people of colour, how many nationalities. True diversity is broader: it's the presence of different perspectives, experiences and ways of thinking.

Equity is about fairness, ensuring that systems don't just look open but actually are accessible. It asks: Are opportunities designed so everyone has a real chance to succeed?

Inclusion is the active work of creating environments where people feel safe to contribute their voice. Foundational research argues that diversity creates value only when organisations enable inclusion.[82] It's the difference between being invited to the meeting and being asked to speak – and truly heard.

For leaders, the trap is to treat diversity as a checklist. The deeper challenge is to create a culture where diversity fuels better collaboration, sharper decisions and greater innovation.

FUN FACT: The power of diversity in numbers

Research from Cloverpop, a decision-making platform, found that inclusive teams make better business decisions up to 87% of the time. Even more striking, those decisions delivered 60% better results.[83] It's not magic – it's maths. More perspectives reduce blind spots and expand options. In other words: diversity isn't just morally right, it's strategically smart.

FUN FACT: Lego's colours

In 1950, Lego sets came in just a handful of colours. Today, they use more than sixty.[84] Why? Because children around the world wanted to build people, homes and stories that looked like their own. Diversity was not an add-on; it became a core part of the brand's identity – and a driver of its global success.

Corporate case stories

The impact of diversity is often easiest to see not in abstract theories but in the lived histories of organisations. Some flourished because they embraced difference. Others stumbled because they ignored or resisted it.

IBM: Building strength through inclusion

As early as the 1950s, IBM took a public stand on equal opportunity, introducing policies against racial discrimination long before it was common in corporate America. Later, IBM became a pioneer in promoting women, LGBTQ+ employees and people with disabilities into leadership roles.[85] These decisions weren't just moral; they became competitive advantages. A diverse workforce helped IBM adapt globally, win government contracts and attract top talent. Their example shows that inclusion is not just a value – it is a business strategy.

Unilever: Diversity driving consumer insight

In consumer goods, diversity is not optional; it's essential to staying relevant. Unilever's campaigns, from Dove's 'Real Beauty' to Lifebuoy's public health initiatives, deliberately reflect a wide range of ages, body types, ethnicities and social realities. Their diverse teams bring perspectives that resonate with consumers across continents. By making diversity part of product design and marketing, Unilever built deeper trust with customers – and stronger commercial outcomes.[86]

Uber: Success without inclusion is fragile

Uber's rapid rise disrupted the taxi industry worldwide. Internally, its culture was plagued by toxic masculinity, harassment claims and a lack of respect for diverse voices. For years, the company prioritised growth at all costs, dismissing early warning signs about the exclusionary environment inside. When scandals broke in 2017, they led to CEO resignation, lawsuits and a reputational crisis that forced Uber to rebuild its culture from scratch.[87] Uber survived as a business, but the episode remains a cautionary tale: neglecting diversity and care can make even the most disruptive companies dangerously brittle.

Médecins Sans Frontières (MSF): Diversity as a human imperative

Outside corporate life, NGOs such as MSF show another face of diversity. Their teams bring together doctors, logisticians, translators and specialists from around the globe, often working in extreme crisis zones.[88] Success is only possible because of the diversity of skills, cultures and perspectives – and because care is placed at the centre. In this case, diversity is not a programme; it is survival.

Lego: Creativity powered by multiple voices

Lego's revival in the 2000s is also a story of diversity. By opening up product development to communities of fans – children and adults from different countries and cultures – Lego crowdsourced creativity on a massive scale. Sets inspired by everything from Japanese anime to NASA space missions emerged, broadening the brand's appeal. By embracing ideas from outside its traditional base, Lego transformed itself from near-bankruptcy into one of the most beloved brands in the world.[89]

The lesson

These cases remind us that diversity is not just a hiring metric, it is also a compass for resilience and relevance. Companies that listen to a broad range of voices create products, cultures and strategies that endure. Companies that silence or sideline difference may enjoy short-term wins – but they build on fragile ground.

Insights from thinkers

If the cases show how diversity plays out in real organisations, these thinkers help us understand *why* diversity so consistently shapes performance, creativity and resilience.

- **Scott Page – Diversity beats ability:** In *The Difference*, Scott Page demonstrates mathematically and empirically that groups of people with diverse perspectives often outperform groups of uniformly high-ability individuals.[90] Different mental models produce better problem-solving, more robust predictions and fewer blind spots. Diversity, in this view, is not charity. It is cognitive horsepower.
- **Amy Edmondson and Henrik Bresman – Psychological safety:** Edmondson and Bresman's research shows that diversity only becomes an asset when people feel safe to speak.[91] Without psychological safety, difference is present but silent. With it, disagreement becomes fuel for learning. Care shows up here as leaders creating climates where voices are invited, not merely tolerated.

- **Rosabeth Moss Kanter – Tokenism vs. Inclusion:** Kanter's work highlights that simply adding minorities to a system does not change outcomes.[92] True inclusion happens when people hold real power, visibility and influence. Diversity without inclusion creates optics. Diversity with inclusion creates transformation.
- **Frans Johansson – The Medici Effect:** Johansson shows how breakthrough ideas often emerge at the intersection of disciplines, cultures and experiences.[93] Innovation accelerates when worlds collide. Leaders who value cross-pollination demonstrate care for possibility, not just efficiency.

Together, these thinkers reinforce what the cases already suggest: diversity is not about looking good; it is about thinking better. It only becomes a strength when leaders pair difference with care, safety and shared purpose.

Care is all around: Diversity in everyday life

When we talk about diversity, it's tempting to think only of corporate programmes or recruitment strategies. In truth, diversity shows its value in everyday life, in traditions and practices that quietly demonstrate how much stronger we become when different voices are brought together.

Take Denmark's tradition of hygge.[94] It's often translated as 'cosiness', but at its heart, hygge is about creating belonging. Candles, shared meals, relaxed conversation – it's less about the objects and more about the feeling that everyone present contributes to the atmosphere. No one dominates; everyone is included. In this way, hygge becomes more than comfort. It's a cultural practice of inclusion, where togetherness itself is the innovation.

Look at Singapore's hawker centres – food markets where cuisines from Malay, Chinese, Indian and Western traditions share the same space. Each stall reflects its own heritage, but the magic is in the mix. People gather at shared tables, often eating dishes from three or four cultures in one sitting. UNESCO recognised hawker culture as a symbol of how diversity isn't abstract policy – it's daily life, made richer through variety, a model of cultural diversity and social cohesion.[95]

Even in more ordinary settings, the same lesson appears. Think of a potluck dinner, where everyone brings a dish, often from their own background. The table is fuller and the meal is more vibrant precisely because no one person dictated the menu. The power lies in the contributions, side by side, each one adding a new flavour.

The lesson for leaders is simple: diversity is not just a metric to measure but a dynamic to live. Whether in culture, cuisine or community, the richest outcomes come not from uniformity but from the care of making space for everyone to bring something of their own.

Challenge the hypothesis

Diversity is often celebrated as an unquestionable good. More diverse teams, the story goes, always perform better, innovate more and deliver stronger results. Is it that simple? Not quite.

Research shows that diversity alone does not guarantee success. In fact, poorly managed diversity can harm collaboration. Without trust, inclusion and care, different perspectives can harden into silos, slow decision-making or even cause open conflict. Leaders who imagine that simply hiring more diverse people is the finish line risk creating frustration on all sides.

There is a difference between being 'at the table' and being *heard* at the table. Organisations sometimes focus on representation – visible diversity – while neglecting the harder work of inclusion. A team can look balanced on paper yet still silence minority voices in practice. True value comes when different voices shape the conversation, not just decorate the org chart.

Diversity goes deeper than nationality, gender or age. It extends to how people think, solve problems and see the world. A team with ten nationalities but identical professional training may think less diversely than a team of three people with radically different experiences. Celebrating visible difference while overlooking cognitive diversity misses the point.

Some companies spotlight their diversity in glossy reports while leaving structures unchanged. This 'diversity washing' can backfire, eroding trust internally and credibility externally. Employees see through empty gestures; customers increasingly do as well. Care means being honest: diversity must be lived, not just advertised.

Diversity creates tension, and that's the point. When managed with care, tension fuels creativity. When neglected, it causes fracture. Leaders must resist the instinct to smooth it away or let it spiral into division. The true work of leadership is to hold the space where difference can become strength.

The hypothesis that 'diversity always leads to better outcomes' doesn't hold without conditions. Diversity is potential, not a guarantee. The care factor is the missing link – leaders must nurture inclusion, welcome tension and create cultures where differences are not just tolerated but celebrated.

In the end, the measure of diversity is not how different people look on the team photo but how deeply they can bring their whole selves into the work. That is where innovation, resilience and trust are born.

When diversity is missing

Think for a moment about what happens when diversity is missing. Conversations feel smoother, decisions come faster, meetings run with less friction. At first glance, it almost seems easier, but underneath, something essential is lost.

Without diversity, teams fall into the trap of seeing the world through a single lens. Blind spots grow unnoticed. Products get designed for 'people like us', while whole groups of customers or communities are left out. Decisions feel confident in the room but collapse when tested in the real world.

It's not just innovation that suffers. The absence of diversity drains resilience. When everyone thinks the same way, mistakes go unchallenged, risks multiply and creativity dries up. Care becomes harder too – because care depends on perspective, on being able to notice the needs of others that don't match your own.

The danger of sameness is subtle. It doesn't announce itself with a crisis on day one. Over time, it narrows vision, weakens trust and locks an organisation into patterns that no longer serve its purpose. That's why diversity isn't a nice-to-have – it's a safeguard against drifting blind.

Next horizon: Designing for deeper diversity

Looking ahead, diversity will not be limited to what we can see – nationality, gender, age or ethnicity. The horizon expands into areas that touch how we think, feel and work.

One such dimension is neurodiversity. Conditions like autism, ADHD or dyslexia are often framed as deficits, but organisations are learning that these differences bring unique strengths: pattern recognition, creativity, hyper-focus or problem-solving skills that others may miss. With care, what once was marginalised becomes central to innovation.

Another rising frontier is intersectionality. People do not belong to just one category. A woman of colour may experience the workplace differently than a white woman, because identities overlap and amplify. Leaders who care must learn to see beyond single labels and understand the layered realities people carry with them.

Then there is the less visible but equally powerful dimension of personality diversity – especially extroversion and introversion. For decades, workplaces have unconsciously favoured extroverts – those who speak up, network and thrive in open offices – but what about those who reflect deeply, create value through listening or prefer to contribute in writing rather than in meetings? The next horizon of diversity may be about designing environments that honour both. Imagine workspaces, collaboration formats and leadership tracks built with different personality rhythms in mind. Care here means not forcing everyone into the same mould but unlocking each person's natural strengths.

Finally, technology adds another layer. Artificial intelligence can personalise learning, suggest adaptive work rhythms and even surface hidden voices in teams – but it also risks amplifying bias if not used carefully. Leaders must navigate this horizon with both courage and caution.

The future of diversity is not about ticking boxes. It is about creating ecosystems where every dimension of human difference – visible and invisible – can contribute to impact. Care becomes the compass that ensures progress does not only move fast but moves fair.

Summary

Instead of generic prompts, we invite you to lean into real dilemmas of diversity.

Reflection questions

- Can you think of a moment when someone's perspective surprised you? Did you lean in or shut down?
- How do you create space for voices that don't naturally push themselves forward?
- Have you ever mistaken sameness for alignment – and missed the value of tension?
- Where might invisible diversity (background, personality, neurodiversity) be shaping your team without you noticing?

Leadership learnings

- Diversity isn't about headcount; it's about how differences work together.
- Tension is not a threat – it's the friction that sparks creativity.
- Exclusion often hides in the everyday: who speaks, who is heard, who is promoted.
- Leaders who embrace vulnerability model inclusion; leaders who cling to control stifle it.
- True care means making diversity more than a programme – making it a practice.

Ask from the author

Diversity cannot remain a slogan, a target or a poster on the wall. It is a responsibility to invite difference, protect it and use it for the greater good.

My ask to you is this: when you feel the pull towards the familiar, resist it. Seek out the voice that unsettles you. Welcome the idea that challenges you. Make space for the colleague whose background is unlike yours. Do not confuse comfort with progress.

True leadership is not about surrounding yourself with echoes. It is about building a table where different voices sit side by side – and ensuring they are heard.

Care in this context is not soft, it is courageous. It demands that you lean into tension, not avoid it. That you let friction spark, not silence it. That you carry the responsibility to make diversity real – not someday but every day, in every meeting, in every decision.

The measure of your leadership will not be how well you led people like yourself but how boldly you created space for those who were different.

INTERLUDE TWO

A LI'L ANTI FABLE: THE BRIDGES ABOVE

In every colony, there comes a time when the walls hum with too much sameness. When even the tunnels begin to wonder if they could bend a little more.

It began with a sound – not the usual rhythm of digging but something lighter. Air whispering where stone used to be.

Li'l Anti followed it to a place where the ceiling shimmered. Through a thin crack, sunlight spilled in like golden syrup.

'The earth is thinning,' said the mason ants.

'Good,' said Anti. 'Maybe the light has something to say.'

No one laughed this time. They were tired of shadows.

Soon after, the Antocrat summoned Anti. 'The colony is growing restless,' he said. 'Find us new ground. Bring back answers – or at least, silence.'

Anti packed a small satchel: a compass carved from seed shell, a page torn from *The Care Factor* and six drops of dew. Then, with a deep breath of his own oxygen, he climbed towards the light.

The world above was loud. Everywhere, ants of impossible colours and customs. One colony traded leaves for honeydew. Another sang their schedules in perfect harmony. A third wore bits of gold and marched in circles, just because it looked impressive. Anti was overwhelmed – and fascinated.

At a central clearing, a group of delegates gathered under a banner of crushed petals: 'Annual Market of Many Colonies'.

A weaver ant bowed: 'We connect our homes with silk threads.'

A cutter ant waved a blade: 'We prune the world into order.'

A farmer ant gestured at a fungus field: 'We feed tomorrow today.'

Anti tried to introduce his concept of care huddles. The others tilted their heads.

'We care,' said the weaver, 'by weaving.'

'We care,' said the cutter, 'by cutting.'

'We care,' said the farmer, 'by feeding what's not yet visible.'

Anti realised something: care wasn't a single act – it was a dialect spoken differently in every colony. That night, he wrote: 'Diversity isn't disagreement. It's the earth trying multiple solutions at once.'

Two days later, Anti reached a colony unlike any he'd seen. Their tunnels gleamed with metal dust; their mandibles clicked in perfect rhythm. At the entrance stood a sign carved in glass: 'The Shiny Ants – Efficiency is Evolution'.

Inside, a massive contraption pulsed and hummed. It sorted seeds faster than any worker could. Screens of reflected sunlight showed rising numbers – production, precision, perfection.

'Your invention is remarkable,' said Anti to their fore-ant. He smiled – the sharp kind. 'It eliminates error. Even the slowest worker now achieves greatness.'

Just then, a squeal. A small worker had slipped into the gears. The machine paused, then continued. No one moved.

'Don't worry,' said the fore-ant. 'We'll make another.'

Anti felt the book press against his side again – heavier now. The words returned: 'Care without conscience is just polished control.'

He left before dawn, the hum of the machine still in his bones.

At the edge of the meadow, Anti found something unexpected: a gathering of ants from many colonies – farmers, weavers, cutters, even a few shiny ones who had walked away. They were building bridges of leaves and silk, spanning streams and cracks. Not for trade, not for conquest – for connection.

'What are you building?' Anti asked.

'Paths,' said one. 'So none of us cross alone.'

He joined them. They worked in silence, each bringing their own way of caring – silk, sap, design, strength. The bridges swayed but held.

As the last leaf settled, the weaver turned to him: 'Your tunnels run deep,' she said. 'But depth means little without reach.'

Anti looked across the meadow – lines of green stretching like veins. Connection wasn't chaos, it was coherence.

That night, under the moon, he wrote: 'Values are the fibres that hold innovation steady. Diversity is the wind that tests the weave. Ethics is knowing which threads to let go.'

When Anti finally returned to the colony, the air felt different. He no longer wanted to command; he wanted to translate. He taught the workers to weave between layers, to share dew from deeper wells. He showed them bridges – tiny at first – between teams, tunnels and temperaments.

Not everyone understood, but something began to shift. Less shouting, more listening. Less digging for volume, more digging for purpose.

Before sleeping, Anti opened the same book that had started it all. Next to the old line – 'Care for self, people, results and values' – he added a new one in moss ink: 'Care for difference, so that results can breathe'.

He smiled. Tomorrow, he would teach them to build their first bridge, not to escape the colony – but to remind it how far light can travel once you stop fearing the cracks.

Leadership commentary

This fable teaches us that care reveals itself not through uniformity but through our ability to engage difference with curiosity ethics and responsibility.

Care factor connection

This fable weaves together the themes of ethics, diversity and innovation explored in Chapters 4, 5 and 6. It reflects the tension leaders face when new ideas, unfamiliar perspectives or technological progress challenge established ways of working.

Leadership insight

The cracks above the colony are not signs of failure – they are invitations. Ethical leadership often begins when a leader dares to follow light rather than simply enforce rules. Curiosity, in this sense, is not rebellion; it is care expressed as moral responsibility.

The Market of Many Colonies reminds us that care is not a single behaviour or language. Different teams, cultures and disciplines express care in different ways. Inclusion, therefore, is not about agreement but about learning to translate between dialects of care so that difference becomes a source of wisdom rather than friction.

The machine of the shiny ants exposes the shadow side of progress. Innovation without empathy may optimise systems but it erodes humanity. Efficiency alone cannot be the measure of success; care must act as conscience, shaping not just what we build but what we are willing to sacrifice – or refuse to.

Finally, the bridge builders offer a model of mature leadership. Sustainable systems do not eliminate difference, they connect it. Shared values become the architecture that allows experimentation without fragmentation. In this way, care functions as trust made visible – not a soft ideal but the structure that holds innovation steady.

Author reflection

Difference often unsettles leaders, not because it is dangerous but because it is unfamiliar. When long-standing patterns begin to crack, the instinct is either to seal the opening quickly or to impose order from above. Both reactions feel responsible. Both are incomplete.

This interlude reflects my own learning that care and ethics rarely arrive as certainty. More often, they arrive as questions – small disturbances that invite us to look beyond what has always worked. Curiosity, in this sense, is not indulgent, it is a moral act. It signals a willingness to engage rather than control, to listen rather than silence.

The bridges Li'l Anti encounters are not built to eliminate difference but to hold it. That distinction matters. Leadership does not require us to resolve every tension; it asks us to create enough trust, shared values and ethical grounding so that difference can be explored without fear. When care becomes connective tissue rather than a rulebook, innovation gains both courage and conscience.

Reflection for the reader

- Where in your leadership does difference currently feel like a disruption rather than a resource?
- Which 'cracks' are you tempted to close quickly instead of exploring more deeply?
- How do you distinguish between efficiency that serves people and efficiency that quietly replaces them?
- What shared values could help your organisation connect difference without fragmenting?

7

Caring In Communities: The Suspension Bridge Of Care

A suspension bridge is one of the most elegant feats of engineering. At first glance, the towers and roadway may seem to do all the work, but the real strength lies in the cables – thousands of thin steel wires, each insignificant on its own, woven together into strands then bundled into ropes. No single wire could carry the weight of cars, trucks and trains. Together, they can span miles.

This is how a community works. Each person brings a different perspective, skill or experience. Alone, those differences may feel fragile – even vulnerable – but when linked they create resilience and strength that no single voice could achieve.

A suspension bridge also does something symbolic: it connects. Two sides that were once separated by distance or danger become accessible. In the same way, diverse communities connect people across divides – of culture, background or belief – to create something larger than themselves.

Here's the paradox: the bridge only holds if every part plays its role. The towers cannot function without the cables; the cables cannot anchor without the foundations deep in the earth. It is the interplay of all parts that makes the structure stand. Communities, too, thrive not by erasing differences but by weaving them together into something strong, balanced and enduring.

A community, like a suspension bridge, is a deliberate act of design. It requires trust, care and maintenance. Neglect a cable or ignore a crack and the whole structure is at risk. When built with attention and care, it not only holds – it carries people forward, together, across distances they could never cross alone.

FUN FACT: The Golden Gate's hidden community

When the Golden Gate Bridge was built in the 1930s, it was considered an impossible task. Fierce winds, dangerous waters and the Great Depression made it a high-risk project. Chief engineer Joseph Strauss insisted on something radical: a safety net suspended under the bridge. It saved the lives of nineteen men who later proudly called themselves the 'Halfway to Hell Club'.[96]

The bridge wasn't just an engineering marvel – it was a community of workers bound by trust, risk-sharing and innovation. Without that care for the people building it, the bridge itself may never have been completed.

Leadership in practice: The espresso machine divide

In the early days of my leadership at this company, it often felt like two separate worlds existed under the same roof. One world lived in the boardroom, where strategy, numbers and shareholder expectations dominated every conversation. The other world gathered around the espresso machine, where people swapped stories, shared frustrations and quietly rolled their eyes at 'management'.

It was more than gossip. These were two communities, each with their own truths, each convinced the other 'didn't get it'. Executives dismissed the coffee-corner talk as complaining. Employees dismissed boardroom debates as being out of touch. I – standing with a foot in both camps – found myself torn.

I remember hearing the same project described in completely different ways depending on where I stood. In the boardroom, it was 'strategic alignment'. By the espresso machine, it was 'yet another top-down decision with no sense of reality'. I kept asking myself: How can both be true? If they are, how do we ever reconcile them?

At times I felt anger rise up when the criticism felt unfair. Other times I felt a creeping doubt: were we as leaders missing something fundamental? The tension pulled me in both directions until I realised the hard truth – I couldn't choose one 'truth' over the other. If we wanted to move forward, we had to find a way to bring these two worlds together.

We started to build bridges. I invited people from the espresso machine into strategy discussions, not as tokens but as contributors. Leaders began spending less time behind closed doors and more time listening – really listening – by the coffee machine. Slowly, suspicion gave way to curiosity. Ideas that had once been dismissed as 'complaints' became seeds for genuine improvements.

The turning point wasn't a single meeting or decision. It was the gradual recognition that both communities carried essential pieces of the same puzzle. When those pieces finally came together, something shifted. The energy in the company changed. The espresso machine stopped being a place of division and became a place where strategy and lived experience met in real conversation.

Looking back, I see now that this was our first step towards becoming a true community: a group of people who not only worked together but who agreed to learn together. That simple shift – from parallel worlds to a shared journey – was what allowed us to move from mistrust to momentum. It all started with acknowledging that both truths belonged.

PARADOX ALERT: The unity of dissonance

The paradox of community is this: the tensions that feel divisive are the forces that can hold it together. Homogeneity feels comfortable, but it is brittle. True community is forged in dissonance – when competing truths, styles and voices rub against each other without splintering apart. Leaders who shy away from that friction may preserve harmony but they lose resilience. Leaders who lean into it discover something stronger: unity that does not erase difference but is sustained by it.

If the espresso machine taught me how to hear the heartbeat of the system, the 'North Korean outputs' showed me what happens when the system stops beating honestly.

Leadership in practice: The illusion of a perfect community

Not all communities are healthy. I once worked with a leader whose team looked, on the surface, like the perfect one. Meetings were orderly. The leader's decisions were praised. Feedback cycles, 360s and formal reviews all painted the same picture: flawless performance.

It didn't take long to realise something was wrong. The team had become a closed loop, telling the leader only what he wanted to hear. Instead of challenging ideas, they reinforced them. Instead of raising concerns, they silenced them. When he proudly showed me his 360 report, the results were spotless – not a single weakness. That was the warning sign. It reminded me less of a high-performing organisation and more of the stories we hear about North Korea, where even absurd myths are repeated until they become 'truth'.

Kim Jong Il was once reported to have played a round of golf with eleven holes-in-one. Everyone knew it was fiction, but no one dared to say otherwise. I felt a similar tension in this team. The spell of compliance was so strong that reality no longer entered the room.

What broke the illusion was not a formal process but the courage of one voice – a colleague who quietly pointed out what was obvious to everyone but never spoken: the emperor had no clothes. Like the child in Hans Christian Andersen's tale, that single moment of honesty cracked the façade. From there, conversations began to shift.

The lesson was clear. Communities that care are not built on flattery or conformity, they are built on truth. Leaders must have the courage to invite real feedback – not just polished praise – and communities must protect the space for dissent. Without that, a 'perfect' community becomes dangerous, blind and brittle.

PARADOX ALERT: The peril of harmony

The more a leader demands harmony, the less healthy a community becomes. What looks like unity can actually be silence, compliance or fear. True cohesion only comes when leaders create space for tension, disagreement and imperfection. A community that dares to question itself is far stronger than one that pretends it has no flaws.

Defining communities

At first glance, **community** can seem like a simple word – a group of people, gathered around a place, an interest or a shared identity. True communities run deeper than proximity or shared labels; they are built on intention and purpose.

As Simon Sinek puts it, 'A community is a group of people who agree to grow together,'[97] emphasising mutual responsibility and trust. That phrase captures two essential truths:

1. **The 'agree':** Communities don't just happen, they are chosen. People make a conscious

commitment to connect, to participate and to contribute.

2. **The 'grow together':** The point of a community is not static belonging but collective progress. Members are linked not only by what they have in common but also by the journey they choose to take side by side.

In organisations, this distinction matters. A workplace can be full of people, but without intention and shared growth it is only a crowd. Communities transform crowds into networks of care, where trust and mutual investment turn colleagues into allies.

For this book, when we write about communities, we are not only describing social groups but also the ecosystems of support, accountability and shared learning that allow both individuals and organisations to thrive.

FUN FACT: The origin of the word 'community'

The word 'community' comes from the Latin *communitas*, meaning 'shared in common'.[98] In Roman times it described not just physical closeness but also obligations to one another – to defend, to celebrate and to care. Over centuries, the sense of reciprocity has remained: communities are never just about being together but about what people give and receive in a relationship.

Corporate case stories

If care is the soil, community is what grows from it. The following cases show what happens when organisations move beyond seeing people as resources and begin treating them as members of something larger.

Patagonia: More than profit

Patagonia, as discussed in Chapter 3, is known not only for its environmental activism but for the community it builds within. Employees surf together at lunch, join grassroots campaigns and share a sense of purpose larger than profit.[99] Patagonia's well is cultural, binding people to values as much as to work, building an internal and external community grounded in shared purpose.

Ben & Jerry's: A community-centred core

Ben & Jerry's has similarly woven community into its DNA.[100] From supporting refugee rights to championing climate justice, they've built a brand where employees and customers alike feel part of a community of values.

Habitat for Humanity: Building communities together

Habitat for Humanity takes the idea of community literally. Volunteers – from local neighbourhoods to international partners – come together to build homes side by side with the families who will live in them.[101] It's not just construction, it's connection. A suspension bridge of care is formed plank by plank as people who might never otherwise meet share tools, sweat and purpose. The result is more than houses, it is communities that stand stronger because they were built together.

The Barefoot College: The bridge of knowledge

The Barefoot College in India brings another dimension: learning as community. Here, rural women – often grandmothers – are trained to become solar engineers, bringing light and power to villages long left behind. These 'solar mamas' not only electrify homes but are empowered to ignite confidence and dignity.[102] The bridge here is not concrete or steel but knowledge, stretching across generations and geographies.

WeWork and online forums: An absence of care

There are cautionary tales. WeWork spoke the language of community loudly, but the culture underneath often rewarded charisma over care.[103] Online platforms like certain Facebook groups or Reddit[104] forums reveal a similar risk: when care is absent, echo chambers form, misinformation spreads and hostility festers. The well becomes poisoned, not nourishing.

Together, these cases reveal a simple but demanding truth: community is never built by language alone. It is built by behaviour. Where leaders invest in shared purpose, dignity and contribution, community becomes a source of energy and resilience. Where care is absent, even the most seductive narratives of belonging collapse into performance, polarisation or exploitation. Community, in the end, is not a branding exercise. It is a living relationship – sustained only by consistent care.

Insights from thinkers

If the cases show community as lived experience, these thinkers help us understand the deeper mechanics of how community is formed, sustained and sometimes broken.

- **Martin Buber — I–Thou relationships:** Buber distinguished between *I–It* relationships (where others are treated as objects) and *I–Thou* relationships (where others are encountered as full human beings). Community, in his view, emerges only in I–Thou space – when people meet each other with presence, respect and mutual recognition. Care is not an add-on; it is the doorway.[105]
- **Elinor Ostrom — Governing the commons together:** Ostrom's research on communities managing shared resources showed that people

can successfully self-organise without heavy central control when they share clear norms, mutual monitoring and collective responsibility. Strong communities don't rely on coercion; they rely on trust, participation and fairness.[106]

- **Brené Brown — Belonging through vulnerability:** Brown's work demonstrates that true belonging does not require people to fit in – it requires them to be seen as they are. Communities grow when leaders model vulnerability, invite honest conversation and create spaces where imperfection is safe. Shame erodes community; empathy builds it.[107]
- **Etienne and Beverly Wenger — Communities of practice:** The Wengers showed that communities form naturally around shared craft and learning. People bond not only around identity, but around doing meaningful work together and getting better over time. Community deepens when contribution is visible and valued.[108]

Together, these thinkers echo what the cases already suggest: community is not created by architecture, perks or slogans. It is created when people are treated as subjects rather than objects, when responsibility is shared, when vulnerability is safe and when contribution matters. In that sense, community is not something leaders build for people. It is something leaders make possible *with* people – through consistent, everyday care.

Care is all around: Communities in everyday life

When we think of community, it's easy to picture neighbourhoods or workplaces. Community exists in many forms, some so ordinary we barely notice them.

In small towns across the Nordics, 'study circles'[109] bring people together to learn. It could be a group of farmers studying renewable energy, young parents exploring literature or retirees diving into local history. The principle is simple: no single teacher but collective learning. Knowledge grows when shared, and the circle itself becomes a community of purpose.

In sports, community is often the invisible force that sustains teams beyond wins and losses. Think of local football clubs where volunteers coach, drive buses and cook meals. The players may come and go, but the web of care around them creates belonging that lasts for decades.

Even digital spaces show this dynamic. Open-source software projects like Linux or Python are built by people who may never meet in person, yet who see themselves as part of something larger.[110] The code is important, but the trust, collaboration, and shared norms are what make it thrive.

These examples remind us: communities aren't defined by geography or hierarchy. They emerge when people choose to share, learn and grow together. Whether around a table, on a pitch or across the internet, care is the thread that weaves them into something lasting.

Challenge the hypothesis

The common belief is that communities are always positive – warm, supportive and life-giving. That's only part of the truth. Communities can just as easily stifle as they can sustain. They can close ranks, silence dissent and enforce conformity at the expense of growth. The danger lies not in community itself but in how it is held together.

Think of a workplace team that has become too close-knit. New ideas aren't welcomed; instead, the group clings to what's familiar. Anyone who questions the norm is quietly excluded. Belonging becomes conditional on sameness. The community feels safe but it is brittle. In the end, this is not care – it is control dressed up as cohesion.

At the extreme, the same forces that make communities powerful can turn deadly. History is filled with tragic examples – from cults that led followers to collective suicide to extremist groups that justified violence in the name of belonging. These are not aberrations from the logic of community but exaggerations of it: the deep human need to belong, untethered from truth or care. When the leader becomes the myth and the group validates the illusion, the community becomes a cage instead of a source of growth.

This is where our analogy of the suspension bridge becomes vital. A bridge stands strong because the cables are stretched – not slack but not pulled to breaking point either. If the cables are too loose, the structure wobbles and collapses. If they are too tight, it loses all flexibility and eventually snaps. Communities work in the same way. When diversity of thought and honesty are stretched across the structure, tension becomes strength. When leaders or groups pull too hard – demanding loyalty, uniformity or blind obedience – the very fabric of community frays and fails.

For leaders, the lesson is clear: communities require not just connection but calibration. Care means asking: Are we creating a space that invites honesty or are we demanding loyalty at all costs? True communities thrive not by suppressing difference but by holding it. They grow stronger by allowing individuals to stretch, to disagree, even to walk away.

When community is missing

If toxic communities are dangerous, the absence of community can be just as damaging – only in quieter ways. Without community, people may not collapse dramatically, but they erode slowly.

In organisations, the absence of community shows up as disengagement. People come to work, do their tasks and leave – but their energy never goes beyond compliance. Innovation stalls because no one feels safe enough to suggest a bold idea. Leaders mistake silence for alignment, when in fact it's indifference.

For individuals, the lack of community can feel like drifting. Isolation is rarely physical anymore – most of us are surrounded by people – but it can be emotional. The meeting where no one asks what you think. The team that never celebrates wins. The quiet resignation of not being seen.

Humans are wired for belonging.[111] Studies link social isolation not only to mental distress but to physical health risks as severe as smoking or obesity.[112] In other words, the absence of community doesn't just weaken performance, it also undermines well-being.

A suspension bridge without cables is just a road hanging in the air – fragile, unsafe and doomed to collapse. In the same way, people without community may still show up, but the structure is missing. The strength that holds everything together comes not from the individual parts but from the connections.

When community is missing, people don't burn out with dramatic flames; they fade out, one by one. Organisations that lose community lose their soul.

Next horizon: The future of communities

The communities of tomorrow will not look like those of the past. While geography once defined who belonged, today purpose, technology and care shape the bonds between people.

The pandemic proved that communities don't need four walls to exist. Online networks now connect people across borders in ways that were once unthinkable. The horizon lies in designing hybrid models – spaces where digital scale meets physical intimacy. Trust is easier to build in person, but reach is greater online. The future will demand both.

From climate movements to patient advocacy groups, communities are forming around missions rather than maps. People no longer ask, 'Who is near me?' but 'Who cares about what I care about?' Organisations that can create spaces for these purpose-driven connections will unlock energy far beyond traditional engagement.

Some of the most exciting experiments are happening where generations intersect. In the Netherlands, student housing projects place young people and elderly residents under the same roof. Students receive affordable rent, and in return they spend time with their older neighbours – sharing meals, teaching technology, simply keeping company. The outcome is mutual enrichment: loneliness reduced, empathy expanded and a community that defies age barriers. These models hint at a future where diversity of age is not a gap to be managed but an asset to be embraced.

Technology will increasingly mediate how communities form. Algorithms can help people find others who share passions or challenges, but they can just as easily build echo chambers that harden bias. The horizon for leaders is not to resist tech but to guide it – ensuring that digital tools build bridges rather than walls.

The question is no longer whether communities will exist – they always will – but what kind of communities we create. Will they nurture or exploit? Will they invite openness or reinforce division? The next horizon of communities will depend less on the tools we use and more on the care we bring to designing them.

Summary

After reading this chapter, reflect on your own views on community.

Reflection questions

- Can you recall a moment when you found yourself in two different 'communities' – perhaps at work, in family or in society – each telling its own version of the truth? How did you navigate that tension?

- Have you ever been part of a group where harmony was prized above honesty? What happened when the 'kid in the crowd' called out that the emperor had no clothes?
- Communities thrive when members choose to contribute. Where in your leadership can you create stronger suspension bridges – ties of trust – so people feel safe to bring their full selves, not just the version that fits in?
- Diversity within communities often creates friction. Do you treat that friction as a warning sign or as the heat that forges something stronger?

Leadership learnings

- Communities are chosen, not assigned. People may belong to the same company, but unless they commit to shared learning and growth, they are not truly a community.
- Truth matters more than harmony. Leaders who silence dissent risk building echo chambers instead of resilient bridges. Care sometimes means inviting discomfort so the structure holds.
- Friction is fuel. Conflict, when handled with respect, can make communities more innovative and adaptive.
- The bridge needs maintenance. Like suspension bridges, communities require constant tending:

repairing broken ties, reinforcing trust and ensuring all voices are carried by the span.

Ask from the author

I have lived both sides of this. I've seen communities split – leadership in the boardroom and employees at the espresso machine – each telling their own version of the truth. I've seen what happens when a leader surrounds themselves only with loyal echoes, like the story of my colleague whose 360-degree review showed 'no flaws'. Both felt convincing in the moment, but neither was real.

What I learnt is this: care means daring to unite the stories, not choose one over the other. It means creating spaces where people can disagree without fear, where the 'kid in the crowd' can speak up when the emperor has no clothes.

Now it's your turn. As a leader, will you settle for comfort – smooth meetings, polite silence and surface harmony? Or will you take on the harder, braver task: to be the architect and caretaker of communities that seek truth, embrace friction and grow together?

This is not optional. The strength of your leadership will be measured not by how well you manage individuals but by how well you build communities that endure – suspension bridges of care strong enough to carry the weight of the future.

8

Caring About Learning And Growth: Where Ideas Buzz And Develop

A beehive is more than a collection of insects; it is a living system. Thousands of bees, each with different roles, move with astonishing coordination. Some gather nectar or protect the hive, others fan their wings to regulate temperature. No single bee sees the whole picture, yet together they sustain life and create honey.

Learning in organisations works the same way. No leader or team can hold all the knowledge. Progress depends on the flow of learning between roles, generations and perspectives. Just as bees dance to signal where flowers bloom, people share insights that guide collective action. Just as bees return with pollen to feed the hive, individuals bring back lessons that nourish the whole.

A single bee is fragile, almost insignificant, but within the care of the hive, its work contributes to something enduring and sweet. In the same way, individual learning without connection often fades, but when leaders create a culture of care, learning compounds, spreads and becomes growth that sustains the entire system.

A hive thrives because every bee plays its part with precision and purpose, but without care for rhythm, coordination and balance, the hive unravels. Care is the invisible thread that holds the swarm together, turning individual actions into collective harmony. Without it, activity becomes noise and the hive collapses into chaos.

FUN FACT: From sweet to hot

Honey itself keeps evolving. Once a simple sweetener, it is now rediscovered in new forms – like 'hot honey', where chilli heat meets ancient tradition.[113] What makes this blend work is care: for honouring the past while daring to experiment, for taste and balance, and for creating something that surprises without losing its roots. Care is what allows tradition and innovation to meet in ways that feel both timeless and new. It is a reminder that learning is not just about preservation but about merging, adapting and creating something fresh.

Leadership in practice: Learning where you least expect it

When Elisabeth and I acquired the farm, it quickly became clear that our executive experience didn't count for much here. The only animals on the farm were bees, a dog and a cat – and we were the ones who had the most to learn.

Elisabeth took the lead on the bees. She signed up for a course, and when the hives arrived, she worked side by side with a seasoned female beekeeper. Patiently, this mentor guided her through the rhythms of the hive: when to intervene, when to leave the bees alone and how to sense when the balance was shifting. Watching Elisabeth in this process was humbling. It reminded me that true growth comes when we accept being the learner, not the leader.

At the same time, a young person began helping us on the farm. He had skills neither of us possessed – taking down trees safely, handling a chainsaw with confidence. Suddenly, Elisabeth and I were the students, learning from someone much younger but far more experienced in the tasks at hand. It wasn't always easy to accept, but it was necessary.

The same lesson showed up at work. Years earlier, I had started a reverse mentoring programme, pairing senior leaders with younger colleagues to exchange perspectives. It sounded simple enough, but it was not an easy sell. Some leaders were sceptical, uncomfortable with the idea of 'being taught' by someone with less tenure. Hierarchy runs deep, and even I had to fight my own instinct to always have the answers, but we pressed on.

When the programme got underway, something powerful happened. My own young colleague didn't just share insights about technology or trends – she challenged my assumptions, broadened my worldview, and in doing so, helped me become a more mindful leader. Slowly, my team began to see it too. They realised that stepping into the learner's seat didn't diminish their authority – it strengthened their ability to lead.

The farm and the office could not have been more different, but the truth was the same: learning flows in all directions. Growth doesn't follow hierarchy, it emerges when we have the humility to listen – to wisdom that comes from age and to fresh perspectives that come from youth.

PARADOX ALERT: Authority vs. learning

The higher you climb, the more people expect you to have the answers, but the moment you pretend you do have all the answers, real learning stops. Teams stop challenging, juniors stop teaching and blind spots grow. Authority feels safest when it projects certainty – yet it becomes strongest when it shows curiosity. A leader who admits, 'I don't know, but I want to learn,' earns more respect than one who always claims to know.

Defining learning and growth

Learning and growth are often reduced to courses, skills checklists or promotions, but at their core they are about transformation.

Learning is the process of expanding what we know and how we see the world. It's not only about absorbing information but about questioning, unlearning and relearning. True learning stretches us – sometimes uncomfortably – and reshapes the way we act.

Growth is what happens when learning takes root. It's the visible change: a new capability, a shift in perspective, a broader horizon of possibilities. Growth is not always upward. Sometimes it means depth – becoming more grounded, wiser or more attuned to others.

The two belong together. Learning without growth risks becoming trivia; growth without learning is unsustainable. Together, they form the engine of personal and organisational renewal.

In this book, I use the definition of learning and growth as the intertwined processes of transformation – where learning expands what we know and growth makes that change visible.

Leadership in practice: Learning as purpose

I have always struggled when I'm sent to a course, a training programme or the like – where you're supposed to embrace the message, incorporate it and run with it. I vividly remember a week-long programme on agile leadership with many good examples from emerging industries. I understood the concept, but when I returned home, nothing happened. Why? Because the part of the industry I worked in was heavily regulated and I was part of a larger system I had no influence on. The context simply didn't allow me to apply what I had learnt.

About a year later, I moved to another country and another part of the company. Suddenly, the same learnings fit perfectly. Now I could use the knowledge I had acquired, and it made a real difference. That experience taught me that learning is not just about what you absorb, but also about when and where it can be activated.

Looking back across my career, I noticed another pattern. The periods when I was most energised, fulfilled and effective as a leader were the times when I was learning the most – and when I was learning together with others. The books, the discussions, the experiments weren't just feeding my curiosity; they were shaping my sense of meaning.

After some deep reflection, I put words to what had been a quiet undercurrent all along: part of my personal purpose is 'learning for life with people I care about'. This wasn't just a slogan, it was also a compass. It reminded me that learning is not only about content or skills, it's also about connection. When I grow, my team grows; when my team grows, the organisation strengthens.

That realisation changed how I approached leadership. I stopped seeing learning as an individual pursuit and started treating it as a collective act. Every coaching session, every workshop, every debrief became more than a task – it became an opportunity to nurture growth together. Purpose turned learning from a personal passion into a shared force.

FUN FACT: Learning curves

The term 'learning curve' first appeared in 1885, when psychologist Hermann Ebbinghaus studied memory and forgetting.[114] He discovered that people forget new information quickly at first, then more slowly over time – unless they revisit it. This became the foundation for the 'curve' we still talk about today.

The fun twist? Modern research shows that forgetting is actually part of how we learn. The act of recalling and relearning strengthens memory more than simply reviewing material.

Corporate case stories

Learning in organisations often carries a formal flavour: training programmes, online modules, certification paths. These have their place, but some of the most powerful learning emerges in less-structured settings – through culture, practice and community.

All Blacks: Humility as daily learning

The New Zealand All Blacks, one of the most successful sports teams in history, are often studied for their skill and strategy. Yet insiders will tell you their true secret is culture. The team lives by a set of principles that shape not only how they play but how they grow together. One of the most famous is 'sweep the sheds'.[115] No matter how big the star, after every match the players pick up brooms and clean the locker room themselves.

On the surface, it looks like a quirky ritual; in reality, it is a daily practice of humility, discipline and shared responsibility. It tells every player: you are never above the team and you are never done learning. Young players see veterans sweeping and the message is clear – excellence is not just about performance under the spotlight but about character when no one is watching.

The result is an environment where learning flows across generations. Older players model humility;

younger players bring fresh energy and ideas. Together they sustain a culture of excellence that has lasted decades. The All Blacks remind us that learning is not an event; it is embedded in the rituals, values and small acts of care that hold a team together.

SodaStream: Learning through experimentation

A decade ago, SodaStream was fading fast. Once known for its quirky home carbonation machines, it was being outpaced by global beverage giants with far deeper pockets. A traditional approach – competing with the same marketing playbooks and product lines – would almost certainly have failed. Instead, SodaStream made learning its strategy.

The company invited employees and even customers into the process of reinvention. New flavours, marketing ideas and product tweaks weren't handed down from headquarters but co-created in fast, scrappy experiments. A bold campaign featured consumers themselves mocking plastic bottle waste. Teams tested ideas quickly, failed often and treated every outcome as data.[116] Learning wasn't a programme run by HR; it was the culture of the business.

The revival was striking. SodaStream repositioned itself not as a quirky alternative to soda but as a fun, sustainable lifestyle brand. Employees describe feeling a sense of ownership because their ideas actually shaped the company's direction. Customers became evangelists, not just consumers. What saved SodaStream was not one big transformation plan but thousands of small acts of learning embedded in daily work. Their story shows how care for experimentation, feedback and shared creativity can breathe new life into an organisation on the edge of decline.

WeWork: The illusion of learning without care

WeWork promised the world a revolution in how we work and learn together. Its co-working spaces were branded as 'campuses', members were told they were joining a 'movement' and leaders claimed that creativity and learning would thrive in their community. The rhetoric was seductive – offices not just as real estate but as ecosystems of innovation.

Beneath the slogans, the culture told another story.[117] Learning was talked about but not practised. Dissenting voices were ignored, critical feedback was suppressed and charisma replaced humility. Teams learnt to mimic enthusiasm rather than question assumptions. Members were invited into the idea of community but decision-making remained centralised, opaque and often reckless.

When scrutiny came, there was no depth to fall back on. Unlike the All Blacks' daily discipline or SodaStream's experiments, WeWork's 'learning culture' was more marketing than reality. Care for truth, feedback and sustainable growth was absent. The collapse that followed was not just financial but cultural: a vivid reminder that you cannot brand your way into being a learning organisation. You have to build it, patiently, with care.

The lesson

Together, these stories reveal a simple but powerful truth: learning is not about programmes or slogans, it is about practice. The All Blacks show how learning can be embedded in rituals of humility; SodaStream shows how it can be fuelled by experimentation and co-creation; WeWork shows what happens when the rhetoric of learning is not matched by care. The conclusion is clear – sustainable growth comes when learning is lived, not branded

Insights from thinkers

Great leaders are often voracious learners, but history shows that depth matters more than volume. Several influential thinkers – past and present – offer perspectives that resonate with our definition of learning and growth as transformation: expansion made visible through change.

- **Confucius: Reflection, imitation, experience** – More than 2,500 years ago, Confucius observed that wisdom comes by three methods: reflection, imitation and experience. Reflection is the noblest, imitation the easiest and experience the bitterest.[118] His words highlight a truth that still holds: real growth requires not just copying others or collecting experiences but reflecting deeply on them. This balance mirrors our definition – learning expands what we know, but growth makes it visible in who we become.

- **Carol Dweck: Growth mindset –** Dweck's research on fixed versus growth mindsets reminds us that learning is not about proving intelligence but about expanding capacity.[119] A leader with a growth mindset sees challenges as opportunities to stretch, rather than threats to competence. In practice, this means welcoming mistakes as part of the process. Leaders who care cultivate environments where people are praised for curiosity, persistence and adaptability – not just for polished results.

- **Peter Senge: The learning organisation –** In *The Fifth Discipline,* Senge described learning organisations as living systems that continually adapt and renew.[120] At their best, organisations become more than machines for efficiency; they evolve into communities where learning is shared, collective and generative. Care is the glue that allows such systems to flourish. Without care, structures for learning quickly collapse into bureaucracy; with care, they become self-sustaining ecosystems of growth.

- **Chris Argyris and Donald Schön: Double-loop learning –** Argyris and Schön distinguished between single-loop learning (fixing problems without questioning assumptions) and double-loop learning (challenging the beliefs behind our actions). This deeper kind of learning is uncomfortable because it requires leaders to confront blind spots and biases, yet it is also the path to transformation. Care makes double-loop learning possible – leaders need psychological safety to question not only what they do, but why they do it.[121]
- **Jack Mezirow: Transformative learning –** Jack Mezirow's work on transformative learning shows that growth happens when people critically reflect on their assumptions and open themselves to new perspectives.[122] Reflection alone is not enough – it requires care. Care creates the safety to question deeply held beliefs without fear of judgement. Care for dialogue allows people to listen rather than defend, to connect rather than retreat. In this way, care becomes the catalyst that turns reflection into transformation – supporting not just individual insight but collective progress.

Across centuries and disciplines, these thinkers converge on a timeless insight: learning and growth are not about accumulation but transformation. Leaders expand when they adopt a growth mindset, reflect deeply, question assumptions and shift perspectives.

Organisations grow when they nurture collective intelligence and systemic renewal. In all cases, care is the condition that makes these shifts sustainable. Without care, learning risks becoming shallow. With care, it becomes the engine of lasting growth.

Care is all around: Learning communities everywhere

Learning communities thrive everywhere if you look closely. Online platforms like Coursera, Duolingo, or edX democratise access to education for millions worldwide. Makerspaces and coding clubs bring people together to learn by building. Language cafés connect strangers who teach each other across cultures.

Even later in life, learning blooms. The University of the Third Age runs programmes where retirees study new subjects together, proving that curiosity has no age limit.[123] Neuroscientists have found that the brain remains plastic well into old age, meaning it can still form new connections and adapt.[124]

Sometimes learning communities emerge in unexpected places. During the pandemic, book clubs, cooking circles and online fitness groups became spaces of shared discovery.[125] People didn't just train their bodies or read novels – they found purpose in growing together when the world felt uncertain.

Organisations, too, have learnt to tap into this power. Open-source communities like Linux show how collaboration without borders can fuel world-changing innovation. Google's famous '20% projects' encouraged employees to explore ideas beyond their job descriptions, seeding products like Gmail.[126] LinkedIn Learning now extends the principle globally, building networks where people learn from experts and from each other.[127]

Seen through the lens of learning and growth as transformation, these examples reveal something deeper. Learning expands what people know – a skill, a perspective, an idea – while growth makes it visible in confidence, resilience and connection. Care is the bridge between the two. It is care that turns an online course into a lifelong habit, a language café into a circle of belonging or an employee side project into a global product. Care makes learning stick and growth possible.

Challenge the hypothesis

We live in a culture that celebrates being 'always learning' – new courses, new podcasts, new certificates – but here's the uncomfortable question: Does more learning automatically make us better leaders?

Consider the bookshelf that grows but never gets read. Or the executive who attends every new leadership programme but never changes how they lead a meeting. Or worse, the leader who jumps on every new trend – agile one month, design thinking the next, AI the month after – leaving their teams confused and exhausted. Learning without integration is like eating without digestion – full but not nourished.

Research backs this up. Cognitive load theory warns that too much input can paralyse decision-making.[128] Studies on unlearning show that discarding outdated habits is often harder – and more transformative – than acquiring new ones.[129] Organisations obsessed with 'failing fast' can burn out teams if they never pause to reflect.

Learning can become a form of vanity – a chase for credentials or novelty that looks like progress but leaves little behind. Growth happens not in how much we absorb but in how deeply we apply, adapt and sometimes let go.

This is where care enters. Care means choosing depth over display, pruning as much as planting. It means giving people the time and psychological safety to stop, reflect and consolidate. Leaders who care don't push teams to learn endlessly; they create rhythms of learning, resting and applying.

Growth is not measured in certificates collected but in lives and organisations transformed.

When care is missing

Learning without care can be as dangerous as no learning at all. Leaders today face an abundance of information, models and trends. Conferences overflow with 'must-have' frameworks; social feeds promise new hacks daily. The risk is that leaders mistake movement for progress.

Imagine a captain with a fast ship but no compass. The crew may work hard, the sails may catch the wind, but without direction the journey drifts. In organisations, the same happens when leaders chase every new idea without anchoring it in care. One month it is agile, the next design thinking, the next artificial intelligence. Teams grow weary, confused and sceptical. Learning becomes noise rather than signal.

Care is what steadies the course. It anchors learning in purpose, ensuring that new methods and frameworks are not just shiny distractions but meaningful tools. With care, leaders ask: Does this idea serve our shared purpose? Does it strengthen us as a community? Does it turn learning into visible growth? Without care, learning fragments. People may collect skills but never integrate them. Energy scatters across projects with little alignment.

Leaders obsessed with learning everything risk learning nothing, but leaders who anchor learning in care and purpose give their organisations the confidence to move together, even in uncertainty. Care does not eliminate storms, it ensures that the journey – however turbulent – leads to somewhere worth going

Next horizon: Learning as shared humanity

The next horizon of learning is not defined by the speed of technology but by the depth of connection. Tools will change, platforms will evolve, yet the essence remains: growth emerges when people learn together.

Communities of learning will matter more than ever. In a world of uncertainty and complexity, no leader can hold all the answers. The organisations that thrive will be those that weave webs of curiosity – across roles, generations and cultures. The future belongs to leaders who see themselves not as providers of knowledge but as gardeners of shared growth.

Technology will play its part, but only as an enabler. What gives learning its power is not the algorithm but the human willingness to care – to share insights freely, to listen deeply, to build resilience together.

The next horizon calls us back to something ancient yet urgently needed: learning as a profoundly human act. When leaders nurture communities of care, they create more than competence. They create belonging, meaning and the capacity to face the unknown together.

One example of this horizon is found in intergenerational learning circles. In several organisations, retirees now mentor apprentices not just in skills but in resilience, while younger employees share digital fluency and fresh perspectives. The exchange is more than knowledge transfer; it is a reminder that growth is communal. What makes it powerful is not speed or scale but care – people choosing to learn with and from one another across divides. This is the horizon of leadership: learning as shared humanity.

This horizon extends beyond organisations. Communities, cities, even nations are rediscovering that resilience lies in shared learning. From climate adaptation projects where farmers swap techniques across continents to grassroots initiatives where neighbours teach one another digital skills, growth comes from care-driven exchange. The leaders who thrive in this future will not be those with the grandest strategies, but those who can create spaces where people listen, learn and grow together. Shared humanity is not a soft idea – it is the most practical foundation for navigating complexity.

Summary

Take this opportunity to reflect on what you have learnt from this chapter.

Reflection questions

- What is one belief you've outgrown? What would it mean to release it fully?
- Where in your leadership are you 'collecting knowledge' without applying it?
- Who could you invite to be your reverse mentor? What would you risk learning from them?
- How does your personal purpose expand when you learn with others, not alone?
- What rhythms of reflection and application could you create so your team's learning turns into growth?
- What truth about yourself have you avoided learning? What might change if you faced it?

Leadership learnings

- Learning is expansion; growth is transformation made visible.
- Unlearning is often the bravest step a leader can take.
- Self-awareness is the hardest learning – and the one that unlocks all others.
- Confidence without curiosity is a blindfold; curiosity with care is a compass.

- Cultures of curiosity outperform cultures of certainty.
- Leaders who learn with others multiply growth across the system.
- Care turns knowledge into wisdom. Learning fills the mind, but only care makes it meaningful. Leaders who rush from one insight to the next may accumulate knowledge but never translate it into wise action. Care slows the pace, asks the harder questions and ensures that what is learnt becomes a guide for others. Wisdom is not found in speed but in the patient integration of lessons lived and shared.

Ask from the author

I have learnt much from books, mentors and experiences, but my greatest growth has come when I humbled myself – when I let go of knowing and embraced learning anew. The hardest lesson of all has been self-awareness. To truly see myself – my blind spots, my patterns, my impact – has been both the most difficult and the most important learning of my life.

That is why my ask to you is simple, but not easy.

Refuse vanity learning. Don't collect certificates; create change. Unlearn the habits that keep you safe but stagnant. Invite younger, different or inconvenient voices to teach you. Anchor your leadership not in being the one who knows but in being the one who grows.

The leaders the world needs now are not the ones with the loudest answers but the deepest questions. They are the ones with the courage to learn, the humility to be taught, the self-awareness to confront their own shadows and the care to grow with others.

The future does not need leaders who simply know more. It needs leaders who care more, who stay deeply human and who can translate knowledge into learning and growth that matters.

9
Caring About Sustainability: Focus For The Future

Sustainability is never a straight line; it lives in cycles. Farmers have always known this. What comes from the soil must be returned to it. Nothing can be wasted without consequence. When that rhythm is broken, the land weakens. When it is respected, the land endures.

In food culture, this wisdom has reappeared in the 'farm-to-table' movement. On the surface it is about freshness, but beneath it lies something deeper – care for the entire cycle:

- **Care for resources** – nothing wasted.
- **Care for people** – knowing where food comes from and trusting the hands that grow it.
- **Care for time** – allowing for seasons, patience and renewal.

- **Care for culture** – preserving traditions while adapting them for the future.

Leadership is no different. When knowledge, practices and resources are treated as disposable, organisations weaken. Quick fixes can fill immediate gaps but they often leave waste behind – burned-out teams, shallow ideas, fractured trust. By contrast, when leaders recycle knowledge, nourish talent and close the loop between past and future, organisations gain resilience.

Sustainability in leadership is not about speed. It is about cultivating cycles of care that keep renewing themselves.

> **FUN FACT: The recycling symbol**
>
> The familiar three-arrow recycling symbol was invented in 1970 by a 23-year-old design student, Gary Anderson, for a competition during the first Earth Day. His design captured a simple but profound truth: everything moves in cycles.[130] More than fifty years later, it remains one of the most recognised symbols in the world – proof that a small act of care, expressed in design, can ripple across generations.

Leadership in practice: The second-hand rug

For much of my life, I bought new and threw away the old. The things I bought were rarely of the highest quality, so when they wore out, they had little value left. That was just how I thought about consumption: replace rather than repair, new rather than lasting.

Elisabeth challenged me on this mindset. She had a different eye, a different way of seeing value. For her, quality lived longer and second-hand didn't mean second-rate. At first it created tension between us – two perspectives on what was worth keeping, what was worth buying.

The turning point came with a rug. Not a new one, but a piece woven in 1965. Its colours carried decades of life, its fabric had outlasted styles and seasons. It was still beautiful, still strong. Seeing it shifted something in me. I began to realise that value doesn't disappear with age – if anything, it deepens.

Since then, we've adjusted our habits. We both buy and sell second-hand pieces now, often of such high quality that they last for decades. We repair, we maintain, and in doing so we join a chain of ownership that extends far beyond us. What's even more striking is how stable the market is for such items. A well-designed table holds its value almost independent of age. Owning becomes not just a matter of style but of financial sustainability too.

The lesson for business is clear. Sustainability is not about endless consumption but about creating things – and systems – that endure. Just as a well-crafted rug or table retains value, so too can organisations when they build with quality, care and long-term purpose. The businesses that thrive are not those that burn through trends and discard their past but those that invest in lasting value, maintain what works and adapt it for new generations.

PARADOX ALERT: The new new

What is old can hold more value than what is new. In our culture of upgrades and fast cycles, it is easy to assume that new is always better, but sustainability often hides in the opposite direction – in the patient care of what already exists. A second-hand rug can outlast a brand-new one of lower quality. A well-crafted table can hold its worth for decades, while the latest design may lose relevance in a season.

Leaders face the same choice. It is tempting to chase novelty and to discard what seems outdated, yet the practices, values and relationships that endure often become an organisation's greatest assets. Sustainability lies not in racing towards the new but in recognising the hidden worth of the old – and having the courage to repair, maintain and adapt it for the future.

Defining sustainability

Sustainability is one of the most used and misused words of our time. It appears on packaging, in corporate strategies and in political speeches. At its heart, the idea is both simple and profound: to meet the needs of the present without compromising the ability of future generations to meet their own. This definition, first articulated in the 1987 Brundtland Report,[131] remains a compass for leaders today.

In business, sustainability is more than environmental responsibility. It is about building organisations that can endure – financially, socially and reputationally. Companies that treat sustainability as compliance often discover too late that stakeholders expect more. Employees want to work for purposeful organisations; customers reward brands that act responsibly; investors increasingly demand long-term value creation. In this sense, sustainability is not separate from business strategy – it *is* business strategy.

When writing this book, I have used the following interpretation: sustainability is the discipline of care expressed across time. It is the ability to act in ways today that make flourishing possible tomorrow – for the organisation, for people and for the planet. Sustainability without care becomes compliance. Care without sustainability risks becoming sentiment. Together, they form a leadership practice that is both human and durable.

To sustain is to care forward. To lead sustainably is to carry responsibility across time – for business, for society and for life itself.

Leadership in practice: Organisational sustainability

One of the things I am most proud of in my leadership journey is helping individuals grow. Many I've coached have gone on to take senior roles, and I count that among the most enduring legacies of leadership. Developing talent, for me, is not optional – it is one of the cornerstones of organisational sustainability.

That was the spirit I carried into a challenge with a colleague who had worked closely with me for several years. This person was energetic, driven and results-oriented. The team delivered, no question, but beneath the surface there were warning signs. The leadership style leaned heavily on control rather than support. Other departments confided that they were hesitant to engage – they didn't want to risk being 'in the way'.

I chose to lean in. I offered feedback, encouragement and coaching. Together with HR, we even engaged an external coach. There were flashes of progress – small steps that gave hope. Gradually the truth emerged: the change was more performance than transformation. At the core, we held different beliefs about leadership. Where I saw leadership as enabling, this person saw it as commanding. Where I valued accountability and collaboration, the focus here was on authority and control.

Eventually we had a direct, honest conversation. It became clear that our paths diverged. We agreed to part ways.

What happened next surprised me. At first, the team wobbled. Some felt disoriented without the old structures of control, but before long, a shift occurred. Freed from the shadow of directive leadership, the majority began to flourish. Initiative grew, trust deepened and a new ecosystem emerged – one where care and sustainable development could take root.

The lesson was stark: organisational sustainability is not only about nurturing talent; sometimes it requires pruning. Letting go of a strong individual can feel like loss in the moment but it can release energy for the many. Care, in this sense, is not indulgence; it is the courage to create conditions where the whole can thrive – even if it means saying goodbye to a part.

PARADOX ALERT: Let it go

Sometimes the most sustainable act of leadership is not to hold on but to let go. Retaining a high performer who undermines collaboration can weaken the whole system. By contrast, releasing control – even at the cost of losing one individual – can unlock growth, trust and resilience across the many.

FUN FACT: Fungi as hidden care

In forests, fungi act as the planet's quiet recycling system.[132] They break down dead matter and turn it into nutrients that sustain new growth. Without fungi, ecosystems would collapse under the weight of their own waste. Their work is rarely visible, yet it is essential. In this sense, fungi teach us something profound about sustainability: care is not always dramatic or glamorous. Often it is the hidden, ongoing work – unseen, uncelebrated – that makes renewal possible.

Corporate case stories

Up to this point, I've shared personal reflections and stories from my own journey. Sustainability is bigger than any one leader's perspective. To see its full force, it helps to look at how companies have succeeded – and failed – in embedding care into their strategies.

The following cases show both sides of the spectrum: bold actions that built trust and growth and shortcuts that ended in collapse. Each offers a lesson in how sustainability becomes either a source of resilience or a risk of ruin.

Patagonia: 'Don't buy this jacket'

On Black Friday 2011, while other retailers pushed discounts, Patagonia ran a full-page ad in *The New York Times* with the words: 'Don't Buy This Jacket'.[133]

The ad featured one of their best-selling products and asked customers to think twice before purchasing. It was a bold move that could have backfired spectacularly. Instead, it cemented Patagonia's reputation for authenticity. Sales actually grew, not because people ignored the message but because they trusted a brand that put the planet before profit.

IKEA: Designing for circularity

IKEA, known for mass-produced furniture, has pledged to become climate-positive by 2030.[134] Beyond lofty promises, they've launched concrete programmes: buy-back schemes where customers can return used furniture for resale and product redesigns focused on durability and recyclability. In one pilot, a chair was built entirely from recycled materials – not only sustainable but cheaper to produce.

Unilever: Sustainable living brands

Unilever's Sustainable Living Plan was ambitious: cut environmental impact in half while improving health and livelihoods for millions.[135] Critics were sceptical, yet the results spoke. Brands most tied to sustainability, such as Dove's 'Real Beauty' or Lifebuoy's handwashing campaigns, became the company's fastest-growing. For Dove, connecting a beauty product to women's self-esteem turned into both cultural impact and commercial success.

The Red Cross: The blood donation loop

Sustainability is not just about products or profits; it is also about systems of care that endure. The Red Cross blood donation network is a powerful example.[136] Every day, countless individuals give a part of themselves, anonymously, for the sake of others they will never meet. The system depends on cycles – continuous donations, careful storage, responsible use – with every step built on trust.

The lesson

Patagonia teaches us that when you align values with action, even counterintuitive choices can build loyalty. IKEA embeds care into everyday products, and sustainability becomes business as usual. Unilever teaches that when purpose drives innovation, sustainability fuels growth, while Volkswagen shows us that sustainability cannot be faked. Deception may deliver short-term results, but once trust is broken, recovery is painfully slow.

The Red Cross teaches us that sustainability is not maintained by one grand act, but by many small, recurring commitments. Just as a blood supply must be renewed constantly, organisations must create cultures where care is practised daily, not only announced in strategies.

Insights from thinkers

No leader invents sustainability alone. The idea has been shaped by voices across decades, reminding us in different ways that care is not optional – it is the only path to endurance.

- **Donella Meadows, Dennis Meadows and Jorgen Randers: Limits to growth –** In 1972, Donella and her colleagues issued a stark warning: unchecked growth would run up against ecological and resource limits.[137] At the time, many dismissed it as pessimism, yet fifty years later her systems thinking feels prophetic. What Meadows offered was not just data but a mindset: caring for limits is not weakness, it is wisdom. Growth without limits destroys itself. What looks like strength in the short term – constant expansion, endless consumption – becomes fragility in the long term. Real resilience comes not from ignoring limits but from caring for them.
- **John Elkington: The triple bottom line –** In the 1990s, John reframed corporate responsibility with his 'triple bottom line' of people, planet and profit, reminding organisations that financial results cannot be separated from social and environmental impact. His message was clear: caring cannot be one-dimensional. An organisation that thrives financially while harming communities or ecosystems is not sustainable; it is burning its own future.[138]

Elkington's framework reminded leaders that real performance requires widening the lens and extending care across domains.

- **Kate Raworth: Doughnut economics** – More recently, Kate Raworth visualised this balance in another image, the doughnut, arguing that true sustainability means operating within both an ecological ceiling and a social foundation.[139] Between the outer ring of planetary boundaries and the inner ring of social foundations lies a safe operating space for humanity. Overshoot the outer limits and the earth is degraded; fall short of the inner ones and people suffer. Focusing only on the planet can harm people, while focusing only on people can harm the planet. Care requires balance – ensuring no one falls short without overshooting our planet's means.
- **Indigenous wisdom: The seven generations principle** – Perhaps the most timeless wisdom predates all of these frameworks. In many Indigenous cultures, decisions are guided by how they will affect the seventh generation to come.[140] This is care across time at its deepest level. It frames leadership not as ownership but as stewardship, a recognition that we hold resources in trust for those who follow. To lead with this mindset is to understand that the measure of sustainability is not today's results but tomorrow's inheritance.

Taken together, these thinkers show that sustainability is not a technical formula, it is a discipline of care: care for limits, care across domains, care for people and planet at once, care across generations. What often looks like restraint, compromise or slowing down is in fact the foundation of endurance. Without this, growth becomes extraction, profit becomes short-sighted and progress collapses into crisis. With it, we build true resilience – systems that last, leaders who endure and organisations that can renew themselves across time.

Care is all around: Building resilience through care

These frameworks may sound lofty but their impact is tested not in board reports but in the small, ordinary moments of everyday life. Sustainability, like care, is most visible in the gestures that repeat daily.

This lesson shows up in business. Ritz-Carlton famously empowers every employee to spend up to $2,000 to solve a guest's problem without asking a manager.[141] Most employees never use the full amount – they rarely need to – but the policy itself sends a signal: care is trusted, not scripted. Empowerment turns customer service from a transaction into a relationship built on respect and discretion.

NGOs know this truth as well. In MSF, sustainability in crisis zones often depends on the smallest routines

– a nurse checking a vaccine fridge temperature, a volunteer carrying clean water, a logistician repairing a generator. These quiet acts rarely make headlines, but they are the difference between collapse and continuity. In extreme conditions, care is the hidden work that makes resilience possible.

Compliance and ethics officers belong in this picture too. They rarely make headlines, but they quietly shape whether these small acts of honesty or dishonesty are tolerated. They are caregivers of trust, ensuring that the little things align with the big principles.

This is how resilience is built in practice: not only through strategies and slogans but also through thousands of repeatable micro-choices – holding a door, sharing credit, enforcing a rule gently but firmly – that compound into trust over time. When care shows up in the everyday, organisations gain a compass they can rely on and a culture that lasts.

The opposite is also true. When care is missing – when shortcuts, neglect or indifference replace these small acts – the compass falters. What looks solid on the surface can begin to crumble from within.

Challenge the hypothesis

Every strong idea attracts its critics, and sustainability is no exception. If we want to build true resilience, we must be willing to test the idea from the inside, not just defend it from the outside.

One challenge is bureaucracy. Many organisations today produce environmental, social and governance (ESG) reports that run hundreds of pages. The data is sliced, coded and colour-graded until the real question gets lost: Are we actually more sustainable than yesterday? The more energy we put into reporting on sustainability, the less energy remains for practicing it. Care risks turning into compliance. We need to measure what matters, but never let reporting replace reality.

Another challenge is the growth debate. Some argue for 'green growth', betting on innovation to decouple economic expansion from environmental impact. Others argue for 'degrowth', insisting that endless consumption is incompatible with planetary limits. Both camps have evidence and both have blind spots. Leaders cannot wait for a perfect answer; they must act in uncertainty, knowing that any choice carries trade-offs. We must lead through paradox – progress often means acting before clarity.

The failures of the so-called 'green economy' are also sobering. Ambitious ventures like large battery factories, wind farms or solar initiatives sometimes collapse under delays, cost overruns or unintended environmental damage. The promise of clean energy can quickly sour if care is reduced to technical optimism without cultural or social grounding. Innovation without alignment is fragility disguised as progress.

On the other side, activist frustration sometimes spills into extremes such as protestors gluing themselves to famous paintings or blocking traffic. These acts may capture headlines, but they also risk alienating the people whose support is needed. Both over-enthusiasm and over-disruption can backfire, creating resistance instead of resilience. While urgency matters, persuasion sustains.

Another challenge is equity. Who pays for sustainability? Is it the consumer in higher prices, the company in lower margins or workers in reduced opportunities? What about global justice – can the Global North continue to demand sustainability standards that the Global South cannot yet afford? If care is unevenly distributed, resilience fractures. Without fairness, sustainability is a castle built on sand.

The point is not to abandon sustainability but to recognise that it is not a finished formula, it is a living practice. Care keeps it alive – not as bureaucracy, not as branding, not as dogma, but as a discipline that adapts to context and evolves with time.

Yet, when that discipline of care is missing – when reporting replaces reality, when branding outpaces action, when equity is ignored – the cracks begin to show. What looks strong in the short term can quietly hollow out, leaving leaders and organisations fragile when it matters most.

When care is missing

If small acts of care build resilience, then small acts of neglect erode it. The cracks often begin quietly: a safety checklist skipped, a report polished to look better than reality, a promise made in public but never kept in practice. Over time, these lapses compound into fragility.

Few failures illustrate this more clearly than plastics in the oceans. For decades, industries promoted single-use packaging as the ultimate convenience, while governments lagged in regulation and individuals consumed without considering the afterlife of what they used. Today, 11 million metric tonnes of plastic enter the oceans every year.[142] Sea turtles mistake plastic bags for jellyfish, seabirds starve with stomachs full of plastic shards and microplastics have now been found in human bloodstreams.[143] What looked like progress – light, cheap, disposable – has become a symbol of missing care. The very materials designed for convenience and durability are undermining the resilience of the ecosystems we depend on.

Another form of missing care is greenwashing – when organisations spend more energy advertising sustainability than actually practising it.[144] A plastic bottle branded 'eco' or 'green' does not erase the waste it creates. The louder the message of care without substance, the faster trust erodes.

Care is also lost in overload. Reporting systems can become so complex that the purpose of sustainability is forgotten. Leaders spend time ticking boxes and publishing glossy reports, while the oceans continue to fill with waste.[145] Care mutates into bureaucracy and the discipline that should sustain becomes the very thing that suffocates.

Sometimes care is missing through indifference. When responsibility for sustainability is outsourced to 'someone else' – another department, another country, another generation – nothing changes. A tree cannot thrive if only one branch receives water, neither can an ecosystem survive when each actor assumes it is another's job to protect it.

What fails in the absence of care is not just sustainability targets but trust itself. Once trust is broken – whether in an organisation, an industry or an ecosystem – resilience is the hardest thing to rebuild.

Next horizon: Building resilience

If missing care erodes resilience, what would a world look like where care was fully present – in our systems, organisations and societies? The next horizon of sustainability is not about doing less harm but about creating the conditions for life to flourish. It is not only about repairing the present but also about preparing the future.

Regenerative leadership is one frontier. It shifts the question from: 'How do we sustain what we have?' to 'How do we restore what has been damaged?' Just as soil can be rebuilt to hold more carbon or forests regrown to balance ecosystems, leadership can regenerate cultures by replenishing trust, energy and purpose. Leaders who embrace this horizon don't just prevent decline; they nurture renewal.

Another horizon is the circular economy at scale. Beyond recycling lies redesign – products, services and systems built so that nothing is wasted. What fungi do in forests, organisations can do in supply chains: transform the end of one cycle into the beginning of another. This requires courage to reimagine business models, not just adjust the margins.

Technology will play a role, but the question is: Will it be technology with care? Renewable grids, AI and biotech could accelerate solutions – or create new crises if ethics are ignored. The horizon is not just innovation itself, but innovation disciplined by care.

Then there is the voice of the future. Some nations already experiment with intergenerational representation – Wales has appointed a Commissioner for

Future Generations, tasked with weighing the impact of decisions on those yet unborn.[146] Indigenous traditions have long practised the same principle: thinking seven generations ahead. This horizon demands leaders who can resist the seduction of quarterly results and instead hold a vision measured in decades.

We must also expand what we count as resilience. Care economies – healthcare, education, caregiving – are often seen as costs. In truth, they are the very infrastructure of endurance. No organisation, community or nation lasts without the resilience built in classrooms, hospitals and homes. The more we prepare only for tomorrow, the less resilient we are today. True resilience is built when the present and the future are cared for together.

The next horizon of sustainability is not a distant frontier, it begins in today's choices – the investments, priorities and habits that determine whether organisations endure or erode. To build true resilience, leaders must see themselves as stewards, not owners, and have the courage to act on behalf of generations they will never meet.

Summary

Take a moment to reflect on what you have learnt in this chapter.

Reflection questions

- Where in your work or life do you see signs of 'small neglects' that could erode resilience over time?
- Which 'second-hand rug' in your organisation might hold more value if it is cared for rather than replaced?
- When do you risk turning sustainability into compliance or branding instead of a living practice?
- How do you balance urgent results with care for the long horizon?
- What role could you play in building resilience beyond your own tenure – for future teams or even future generations?

Leadership learnings

- Sustainability is not a side project; it is the foundation of survival.
- Greenwashing destroys trust faster than silence – authenticity is non-negotiable.
- Loops of care – reuse, renewal, restoration – create resilience where linear thinking creates fragility.
- Care is often invisible and unglamorous, yet it is what holds systems together across time.

- True resilience comes when leaders act as stewards, not owners – investing in people, cultures and ecosystems that will outlast them.

Ask from the author

Sustainability is often framed as a technical problem, but at its core it is a test of leadership. The question is not whether you care in theory but whether you act in practice. Every choice – to repair or replace, to nurture or exploit, to take shortcuts or build for the long term – is a decision about the future you leave behind.

My ask is this: step forward. Refuse the easy path of greenwashing or delegation. Make care visible in your decisions, even when it costs more, takes longer or feels inconvenient. Lead by example in the unglamorous, everyday work that builds resilience – because if leaders do not choose care, no one else will.

History will not remember our slogans or our reports. It will remember whether we left systems stronger or weaker, whether our choices made collapse more or less likely. The time to act is not later, when it is safe or easy, the time is now. Building true resilience starts with you – today.

INTERLUDE THREE

A LI'L ANTI FABLE: THE LIVING BRIDGE

In the weeks after the Bridges Above, the colony felt different – not louder, just… softer around the edges. Lines still formed, work still flowed but the tunnels carried a new kind of sound: a listening.

Li'l Anti noticed how the air moved now. Fewer orders, more signals. Fewer speeches, more glances. Care had stopped being something to announce; it had started to move like water around stones.

Still, questions tugged at Anti: What holds when we are not looking? What happens to care when it's nobody's turn to perform it?

He woke early and walked towards the quietest chamber – the one that breathed. The farmers' garden spread in terraces of white threads and dark soil. Here, the colony's future was tended, not told. Brood and fungus. Water and breath. The ordinary alchemy of survival.

'Care is not a policy,' the farmer had told him once, wiping dew from her antennae. 'It's a cycle. It either completes or it breaks.'

The day the storm came, Anti learnt what she meant.

It started as a tremor, then a hush, then a weight on the world. The ceiling sighed. The air turned metallic. From the crack above – the one that had once poured light like honey – a line of mud began to slip.

'Brace!' shouted the mason ants. 'Routes B and D – clear!' Workers pivoted instinctively. Not towards the centre, but outwards, towards the edges where collapse begins.

Anti ran to the farmers' chamber. Threads had snapped; the fungus leaned, delicate as breath. He put his body under the sagging shelf until others arrived, their legs a forest of resolve.

The colony didn't scream. It rearranged. Teams that had never shared a tunnel now shared a task. The cutters trimmed dead roots to lighten the load. The weavers laced emergency braces. Scouts sprinted through new corridors, marking safer paths with the sharp sweetness of pheromone.

At the narrowest passage, the earth had slumped into a gap too wide to jump. The first ant down hesitated. The second did not. She hooked her legs into the stone, bent her body into the empty space, and waited.

Another ant latched to her. Then another. A living bridge began to grow – trembling, then steady, then sure. They did not argue about whose turn it was. They became the thing that was needed.

Anti stepped onto them lightly, carrying a sliver of fungus like a lantern. Halfway across, he felt it: not just strength but trust. The entire colony balanced on a promise made without words – I will hold so you can pass.

By nightfall, the storm rolled away. The tunnels exhaled. Everyone was tired and everyone was alive.

'Write it,' the farmer said, settling the fungus back into breath and shade. Anti nodded, moss ink pooling in his heart. He wrote: Care is infrastructure we can't see until it carries us.

In the days after, something else shifted. The pheromone trails – once straight and stubborn – became curious. Scouts tested small detours. Foragers placed a crumb here, then there, watching which path kept air drier and feet lighter. Masons charted the micro-cracks where rain had searched for entry. Weavers experimented with a new weave that flexed without breaking.

No council decreed this. The colony learnt by listening to its own movement.

Anti walked alongside the scouts. 'How do you know when a route is right?' he asked.

The scout rubbed her antennae against the ground. 'The ground tells us,' she said. 'And so do you.' She didn't mean him personally, she meant everyone. The pattern of traffic. The weight of a thousand decisions – none heroic, all honest.

At the old intersection where the shiny ants once preached about perfection, they left a small sign in seed shell: We don't eliminate error, we adapt faster than it can grow.

He wrote again: In a caring system, information is oxygen. If it can't breathe, nothing can grow.

Weeks turned to a season. The garden brightened. The brood swelled – tiny commas of tomorrow. The air steadied into a rhythm Anti recognised from the bridges but had never heard underground: continuity.

He spent more time with the older workers now. The ones with blunt mandibles and patient eyes. They taught him the secrets of enough – when to harvest and when to leave. Which fibres held in wet weather. How to return scraps to soil instead of pride.

'Legacy is not what you leave,' one of them said, rolling a kernel towards the nursery. 'It's what you refuse to take.'

During a night inspection, Anti paused by the living bridge, now woven into the architecture itself – reinforced, yes, but also remembered. New workers traced it with their antennae, a ritual of gratitude. The bridge hummed back: a tendon in the body of the colony.

He thought of the old slogan – *Care is productivity* – and felt a small, kind smile. Care was no longer a banner, it was a body – a way the colony had become itself.

He wrote: Sustainability is care extended through time. It's the decision to keep choosing each other.

One dawn, the air changed again. Not heavy, this time. Buoyant. From deep inside the nursery, a tremor of purpose rose into the tunnels – an old pulse that visits only when a colony is ready to test the sky.

Alates stirred: winged ants, soft and new, stirring like seeds that had learnt the grammar of wind. Workers gathered in a circle – not to command but to witness.

'Will they remember us?' a young worker whispered. 'Not by name,' said the farmer, smiling with her eyes. 'By pattern.'

Anti stood beside her, feeling the room breathe. Everything the colony had practised – the bridges, the learning, the balance – would now be translated into flight. Not all would survive, but that was never the promise. The promise was continuity.

He stepped forward and touched a wing with one antenna, a blessing he had never learnt but somehow knew. 'Carry the pattern,' he murmured. 'Carry the care.'

The sky answered with a thin blue note. The crack that once poured honeyed light opened again, and the alates rose – a murmuration of possibility, a constellation of futures. The colony watched, then returned to their work, no less grounded for having looked up.

Anti's last line of the season wrote itself: When care evolves, it grows wings, not to escape but to extend.

Leadership commentary

This fable teaches us that care becomes real when it moves from intention into structure – when it is practised so consistently that it holds, adapts and continues even without direct leadership.

Care factor connection

This interlude deepens the themes explored in Chapters 7, 8 and 9, where care is expressed through community, learning and sustainability. It explores what happens when care is no longer dependent on individual effort or leadership presence but is embedded into how the system responds under pressure and over time.

Leadership insight

The storm does not create the living bridge – it reveals it. In moments of strain, organisations discover whether care exists as language or as readiness. When people instinctively coordinate, adjust and support one another without waiting for instruction, care has become infrastructure.

The living bridge itself is a powerful leadership image. No single ant is heroic; the strength lies in mutual commitment. This is what caring communities look like under pressure: people becoming the structure together. Leadership, in this sense, is not about directing action but about creating the conditions where trust and coordination emerge naturally when they are most needed.

As the colony listens and learns after the storm, care shows another dimension – adaptive intelligence. Information moves freely, feedback is acted upon quickly and experimentation replaces rigidity. Learning is no longer an initiative; it is how the system breathes. Caring leaders protect this flow by rewarding curiosity, signal-sharing and adjustment over certainty and control.

The wisdom of the older workers introduces care as restraint and renewal. Sustainability is not achieved through relentless growth but through conscious choices of 'enough'. Leaders who care design cycles that return value to the system – to people, resources and future capability – rather than quietly depleting them.

Finally, the emergence of wings reframes leadership legacy. What continues is not the leader's presence but the pattern they leave behind. Culture reveals itself in what can be trusted to move forward without supervision. Care has truly scaled when it no longer requires the leader to be there – when it has become continuity rather than control.

Author reflection

We talk about culture as if it were a slogan or a strategy. It isn't. It's a body – a living system of signals, confidences, rituals and refusals. In a crisis, the body shows you what it truly believes. In calm, it shows you what it can sustain.

The living bridge is not a miracle; it is practice, remembered. The wings are not a departure; they are continuity, entrusted.

Care scales when it stops needing your presence to persist. That's when you know it has become infrastructure – invisible, reliable and ready to carry more than any one of us can.

Reflection for the reader

- Where in your organisation do you need a living bridge – a place where people can become the structure together?
- What would it take to let information breathe, so learning moves faster than error?
- Which cycles in your work complete? Which ones quietly break?
- Which part of your culture is ready to grow wings – to continue without you?

10
From Care To Hope: Be The Lotus

In Buddhism, the lotus flower is a symbol of resilience and awakening. It grows not in clear water but in mud. Its roots are buried in the dark, its stem rises through murky depths, and only then does it bloom into the light.

Care is like the mud and the water – not always pretty but essential for growth. It's the context we hold, the nurturing presence that makes it possible for life to continue. Hope is the flower itself – fragile at first, but reaching towards the sun, a visible promise that beauty can emerge from difficulty.

As leaders, we need both. If we deny the mud, we deny reality. If we lose sight of the bloom, we lose direction. Care without hope gets stuck in the dark. Hope without care never takes root. Together, they remind us that even in challenging conditions, something remarkable can grow.

PARADOX ALERT: The bystander effect

When many people are given the opportunity to care, no one actually does. Psychologists John Darley and Bibb Latané called this the bystander effect: the more witnesses there are, the less likely it is that anyone will step forward. Each assumes someone else will take responsibility – and in the end, nothing happens.[147]

For leaders, this is a cautionary tale. Care without action quickly turns into silence. Hope cannot survive if everyone waits for someone else to move. True leadership means breaking the spell – being the one who steps in, and by doing so gives others permission to follow.

Here is the hopeful twist: just as inaction can spread, so can action – because hope, like fear, is contagious.

Leadership in practice: When care turns to hope

I had worked closely with a colleague for more than three years. We had built trust, delivered results and shared the everyday rhythm of leadership. Then, one day, I received news from his partner: there had been an accident.

The message hit me like lightning. I remember standing still, unable to process it at first and then being overwhelmed by a sinking feeling: Is he going to leave us? What about all the 'silent things' he had always brought with him – the good mood, the perspective, the subtle lift he gave to the whole workplace? Why hadn't I noticed them more clearly before?

The recovery process was long, and it changed everything. I got to know him in new ways, and I also got to know his partner – someone I had never met, despite us having worked side by side for years. In those months, I learnt as much about care as I did about leadership: sometimes it is not about performance but about presence, not about goals but about being there.

Slowly, hope entered the picture. Recovery milestones became shared victories. Small steps forward created energy. What had started as a terrifying shock evolved into a journey of resilience and rediscovery – for him, for his partner and for all of us at work.

Looking back, I see how easily we take the 'silent things' for granted in the busyness of organisational life. It should not take a crisis to open our eyes to what really matters. Care gives us the ability to notice them. Hope allows us to believe that they will endure, even when tested.

Please don't wait for an accident to happen to realise what you already have around you.

As leaders, our responsibility is not only to notice and protect what matters, but also to create hope that it can grow again, even after setbacks. That combination makes people – and organisations – truly resilient.

> **FUN FACT: Hope is contagious**
>
> Researchers at Harvard have shown that emotions spread – positive and negative – through social networks much like viruses.[148] When one person expresses optimism, encouragement or belief in a better outcome, it can ripple outward and raise the resilience of an entire group. The same is true for negativity – it spreads just as easily.
>
> The lesson for leaders is simple: hope multiplies when it is shared. A single voice of belief can shift the energy of a room, a team or even an organisation.

Defining care and hope

Care is what grounds us in the present – the attention, responsibility and discipline that keep systems alive.

Hope is what stretches us towards the future – the belief that renewal is possible, that change can take root even when today feels fragile.

The two belong together. Care without hope becomes maintenance, a slow exhaustion of effort. Hope without care becomes an illusion, words without practice. When care and hope work together, they create resilience that holds through crisis and inspires beyond it.

Leadership is tested at this intersection. It is easy to care when things are going well and hope when the future looks bright. The challenge is to care when it feels unnoticed and to hope when outcomes are uncertain. That is where leaders set the tone for cultures that endure.

Leadership in practice: When the team looked back

I once had to announce to my leadership team that we had decided to part ways with one of their colleagues. The message was difficult, and I knew it came as a shock to them. It was my responsibility to carry the decision and to make sure the team could move forward, but it weighed heavily on me as well.

The day after the announcement, one of the team members came to my office. He told me that he and the others had been talking. They realised how hard this must have been for me, too. Then he said something I will never forget: 'We want to apologise for not checking how you were doing in all of this.'

It was a simple gesture, but it meant a lot. In that moment, the flow of care reversed. It wasn't only me looking after them – they looked after me. From that act came hope: hope that our leadership culture was strong enough to hold both accountability and empathy at the same time.

It still moves me when I think about it because it was also a confirmation that we had truly built psychological safety. Real leadership is not about seeking sympathy – it is about creating the kind of trust where care flows in both directions.

PARADOX ALERT: When care weakens hope

Too much care can sometimes dampen hope. As leaders, we often want to protect our teams from pain, setbacks or failure. It feels like the right thing to do – and in the short term, it might even be comforting.

Overprotection carries a hidden message: 'I don't believe you can handle this.' That message undermines resilience and leaves people less prepared for the inevitable challenges that leadership and life bring.

Hope, by contrast, is not built in comfort zones. It grows when people discover that they can carry more than they thought, when they stumble but get back up, when they face the difficult and find strength in themselves and in others.

The paradox, then, is that if we care too much in the wrong way – by shielding others from every discomfort – we may actually suffocate the hope we want to nurture. True leadership lies in balancing empathy with belief: to show care and to signal trust in people's ability to endure and grow.

Perhaps that is why even the earliest civilisations tried to anchor care in something bigger than themselves – a way of ensuring that hope would not be lost.

FUN FACT: Hammurabi's code

One of the oldest known legal codes, Hammurabi's Code (circa 1750 BC), carved laws into stone for all to see. Among its 282 rules were principles of fairness, responsibility and care – including protections for widows and orphans and guidelines for just trade.[149]

What's striking is that these rules weren't only about punishment; they were about creating hope in a fragile society. By making care a collective duty, Hammurabi anchored stability in a time when life was unpredictable and often brutal.

It's a reminder that for thousands of years, leaders have tried to formalise the link between care and hope – not leaving it to chance, but making it a foundation for resilience.

Corporate case stories

Throughout this book, you have encountered stories of care in action, moments where leaders chose courage over comfort, presence over avoidance and responsibility over convenience.

In this final chapter, there are no new corporate cases.

Instead, this is an invitation.

Take a moment to look back at the case stories you've already read.

- Where did you notice hope explicitly shaping decisions, behaviours or outcomes?
- Where was care present, but hope perhaps missing or left unspoken?
- How might those situations have evolved differently if hope had been made visible, named and actively practised?

Now turn your attention to your own organisation.

- Where have opportunities for hope been overlooked?
- Where did people sense that something better was possible, but no one articulated it?
- What small acts of courageous leadership could have changed the trajectory?

Hope rarely announces itself loudly.

More often, it appears as a quiet inner knowing that something can be better, if someone is willing to take the first step.

Perhaps that someone is you.

Insights from thinkers

As this journey draws toward reflection, it becomes clear that beneath all the tools, cases and practices lies a quieter force shaping leadership from the inside out: hope.

- **Václav Havel: Hope as orientation –** The Czech playwright and statesman Václav Havel described hope not as naïve optimism but as 'an orientation of the spirit, an orientation of the heart'.[150] Hope, in his words, is not the conviction that something will turn out well but the certainty that something makes sense, regardless of how it turns out. Hope has its deepest roots not in sunny forecasts but in the soil of uncertainty and even despair. Care, then, is the choice to embody this orientation – to act as if meaning can be made, even when outcomes are uncertain.
- **Barbara Fredrickson: Emotions that build –** Psychologist Barbara Fredrickson's 'broaden-and-build' theory shows how positive emotions such as hope expand our awareness and build enduring psychological and social resources.[151] Teams that share hope together become more resilient in facing challenges. The paradox here is subtle yet profound: emotions often dismissed as 'soft' are the very forces that create the hardest, most durable forms of resilience. Care in leadership means cultivating these emotions deliberately, knowing that hope is both fragile and strong at the same time.
- **Desmond Tutu: Light in the darkness –** Archbishop Desmond Tutu often reminded his

> audiences that 'hope is being able to see that there is light despite all of the darkness.'[152] His words were not sentimental; they were forged in the long struggle against apartheid. Hope shines brightest not when circumstances are easy but when they are hardest. To care as a leader is to help others see that light, to kindle it in the midst of collective difficulty and to act as if it were already guiding the way.

Together, these perspectives remind us that hope is not a luxury or a soft afterthought. It is a discipline of the spirit, a builder of resilience and a light that shines precisely when it seems least possible. For leaders, the message is clear: to care is also to cultivate hope – not only in ourselves but in those around us. When hope is cultivated, it rarely stays confined; it spreads, often in unexpected ways.

Care is all around: Small gestures bring big hope

Care isn't always grand or heroic. Often, it hides in the smallest of gestures that ripple outward – and with them, bring hope.

In Italy, cafés have long practised the tradition of *caffè sospeso* – 'suspended coffee'. A customer pays for two coffees, drinks one and leaves the other for someone who cannot afford it. It is a simple, almost invisible act of care, but for the person who receives it, it can mean dignity, belonging and hope that generosity is still alive.

Look at Denmark's cycling culture, where drivers instinctively pause and wave cyclists through intersections. It's not a law – it's a norm, a shared understanding that safety and flow matter for everyone.

In leadership, too, care is not just in the big strategies but in the micro-moments: a check-in before a meeting, an acknowledgement of effort, a pause to listen deeply. These are the cultural equivalents of a suspended coffee or a waved-through cyclist. They may seem small, but they shape the entire system of trust – and they remind us that hope often arrives in the smallest, simplest gestures.

If hope can be found in the smallest of gestures, we must also ask: What happens when it is absent or when it is replaced with empty promises? To care as a leader is not only to notice where hope exists but also to question where it is missing – and why.

Challenge the hypothesis

Hope is easy to dismiss. Some argue it is little more than optimism dressed up in nicer clothes – too soft for the hard realities of leadership. In some cases, they are right. False hope can be dangerous. We see it in corporate greenwashing, where promises of sustainability mask business as usual. We see it in performative care programmes, where slogans about belonging hide cultures of burnout. When hope is shallow, it erodes trust rather than builds it.

Yet this fragility is what makes authentic hope so powerful. Genuine hope does not ignore difficulties; it acknowledges them and still insists on moving forward. I often remind my teams that hope is not a strategy – and it isn't. Without action, hope collapses into wishful thinking. When leaders pair hope with care and concrete steps, it becomes something far stronger: the fuel that keeps people moving even when the path is steep.

Hope becomes credible not when everything looks bright but when it refuses to die in the face of challenge. Leaders who embody this kind of hope offer something more than a vision – they offer a reason to believe that care can endure, even under pressure.

When care is missing

If authentic hope is powerful, it is also fragile. History shows us how quickly hope can collapse when care is missing. During the Cold War, much of the world lived under the shadow of nuclear threat. A single misstep could have erased hope for an entire generation. Yet even in that darkness, fragile gestures of care – from cultural exchanges to painstaking diplomatic talks – created space for hope to survive.

The same dynamic is visible today. Armed conflicts,[153] authoritarian backsliding and climate anxiety[154] erode trust in institutions and make hope feel out of reach. The greater the fear, the more fragile hope becomes – and yet, the more essential it is.[155] We see this in the courage of those who refuse to give in to despair: communities rebuilding after war, young people marching for climate justice, neighbours helping one another in times of crisis.

For leaders, the warning is clear. To speak of hope without demonstrating care is to build on sand. When care and responsibility are visible – even in the smallest of actions – they create the conditions in which hope can endure.[156] Fragile as it may be, hope remains the most renewable resource we have, provided we do not take it for granted.

Next horizon: Cultivating hope

Hope, then, is not an abstract concept but a practice – something we nurture, protect and pass on. If care is the soil, hope is the seed that grows in it. Like any seed, it requires tending. Left unattended, it withers; given attention, it flourishes and multiplies.

The next horizon of leadership is not only about solving today's problems but cultivating the conditions where hope can continue to grow tomorrow. This means acting with care even when outcomes are uncertain, naming realities without slipping into despair and choosing to see possibilities where others see only dead ends.

Hope cannot be commanded – it cannot be decreed in a strategy or mandated by a slogan. It must be lived, modelled and shown in small, persistent ways. Often this modelling is raw: leaders admitting they do not have all the answers, acknowledging setbacks or showing care even when they feel stretched thin. Yet it is precisely in these moments of honesty that hope takes root because people recognise it as real.

The horizon ahead will not be without turbulence. If care has been the compass of this book, then hope is the direction it points toward: a reminder that leadership is not about guaranteeing outcomes or shielding people from uncertainty but about walking with them through it – and ensuring the journey remains worth taking.

INTERLUDE FOUR

A LI'L ANTI FABLE: THE RETURN OF CARE

The rains had finally come, and with them a silence Li'l Anti had never known before.

The hill stood taller now, the soil darker and richer from seasons of struggle. The scars of the old tunnels still traced faint lines beneath the surface – reminders of storms, mistakes and lessons buried deep.

From the ridge above, Li'l Anti watched the colony move. Young ants – small, curious, endlessly alive – darted between grains of soil, carrying fragments of leaf and seed. Their rhythm was different now – quieter, wiser. Somewhere in their pace, he recognised a reflection of his own journey.

He was no longer the smallest. He no longer needed to prove that he belonged.

The Queen had grown frail, her voice softer, and the elders now turned to Li'l Anti when new plans were whispered.

There was talk of expansion – of new hills beyond the wet fields – and this time, it was Li'l Anti they asked to lead the expedition.

He hesitated. He remembered the long season of division – when care had seemed too slow, when impatience had felt like courage. He remembered the day they almost lost the colony – not to the flood but to each other.

He had learnt then that leadership wasn't about the path taken but about how many hearts walked it together.

That night, before giving his answer, Li'l Anti walked the tunnels one last time. He brushed his antennae against the rough walls, feeling the layered history in every curve – the work of thousands of unseen efforts.

He paused by the chamber where they once stored the seeds that saved them through the drought. He could still feel the warmth of care that had built this place – not the kind spoken about in meetings but the kind that moved silently from one ant's gesture to another's survival.

At dawn, he returned to the Queen. 'I will go,' he said. 'But not to lead ahead – to walk with.'

When the expedition set out, the air shimmered with the smell of new soil. The young ants carried their future on their backs, and Li'l Anti walked among them.

He no longer shouted orders. He listened, adjusted, encouraged.

In that simple rhythm – the sound of thousands moving together – he felt something shift inside him. For the first time, he didn't feel small, he felt connected.

That, he realised, was what leadership truly meant.

Leadership commentary

This fable teaches us that mature leadership is not about leading ahead but walking with – translating care into continuity, succession and shared ownership of the future.

Care factor connection

This closing interlude reflects the later chapters of *The Care Factor*, where care is expressed through transformation, responsibility and long-term stewardship. It brings Li'l Anti's journey full circle, shifting the focus from personal insight to collective continuity.

Leadership insight

By the time Li'l Anti is asked to lead the next expansion, the question is no longer whether he is capable. It is whether leadership will repeat old patterns or evolve into something more relational and enduring.

His hesitation is telling. Leaders who have learnt to care deeply understand the cost of moving too fast or too far ahead. They remember moments when impatience masqueraded as courage, and when results were achieved at the expense of connection.

Choosing to 'walk with' rather than 'lead ahead' marks a quiet but profound shift. Authority gives way to presence. Listening becomes as important as direction. Leadership becomes less about setting the pace and more about sensing the collective rhythm.

This interlude reminds us that care ultimately returns as responsibility for what continues after us. True leadership is measured not by expansion alone but by how many people feel carried, capable and connected along the way. When care is fully integrated, leaders no longer need to prove they belong. They belong – because they have helped others belong too.

Author reflection

There is a quiet moment in leadership when proving yourself no longer matters. What matters instead is what continues – and who feels carried into that future.

This interlude speaks to that moment. The return of care is not a return to softness or nostalgia; it is a return to responsibility. Mature leadership is less concerned with being followed and more concerned with whether others can walk together once you step back.

I have learnt that walking with people requires more restraint than leading ahead of them. It asks us to slow our certainty, to listen longer than feels efficient and to trust that strength grows through shared movement rather than command. Care at this stage is no longer something we practise for effect. It becomes something we protect so it can outlive us.

When leaders stop needing to be central to progress, care has done its deepest work.

Reflection for the reader

- Where in your leadership are you still walking ahead when it may be time to walk with?
- What would continuity look like if your presence were removed tomorrow?
- Which people or capabilities need more trust – not more direction – to grow?
- How are you preparing others to carry the work forward without you?

Conclusion: The Quiet Power Of Care

When I began writing *The Care Factor*, I believed it was a book about leadership. I now realise it is equally a book about life.

Every decision we make as leaders – whether about strategy, people or principles – leaves a trace. Over time, those traces form the culture we inhabit. Some are visible: results, targets, performance curves. Others are silent but far more enduring: trust, belonging, meaning.

Leadership, at its core, is the art of choosing which traces to leave behind.

We started this book by exploring care through the lens of results – because care is often misunderstood as something soft, peripheral or secondary to performance. Yet as we've seen, the opposite is true. When leaders integrate care into how they think, decide and act, results become not only stronger but also more sustainable.

Care, practised well, is not a mood – it's a method.

Leadership in practice: The interview that became a lesson

A few years ago, I was leading an assessment panel for a critical senior role. We had assembled an extraordinary panel – experienced, respected and frankly hard to get into the same room at the same time.

Ironically, the one candidate we met when the full panel was finally present was the most junior of the entire group. It quickly became clear that the role was too big. The presentation was structured, the business case sound but the delivery hesitant. We were running ahead of schedule – fifteen minutes early, in fact – and could easily have ended the session politely and moved on.

Instead, we paused. I asked the panel if, before closing, they would share a few personal reflections: 'If you were stepping into this role tomorrow, what would you actually focus on?'

It was as if the room exhaled. The tension of evaluation gave way to reflection, and suddenly everyone was speaking not as assessors but as leaders sharing what they'd learnt the hard way.

One by one, the senior leaders began speaking – not in corporate clichés, but with honesty and humility. They spoke about the gap between plans and reality, about listening before acting and about the importance of earning trust early.

One of them said something that stayed with me: 'The plan is important because it forces you to think. When it's time to implement, you have to almost scrap it – and focus on the people.'

The candidate left that room knowing the role wasn't theirs, but they also left with their head high, inspired by what they'd just witnessed. A moment that could have been deflating turned into something affirming – for all of us.

It reminded me that care in leadership isn't about protecting people from the truth. It's about how we tell the truth – and the dignity we give others in the process.

Leadership in practice: The poems of goodbye

There are teams you work with and there are teams that shape you. This one had done both.

We had lived through crisis together – the kind that tests not only competence but character. We had disagreed, struggled, laughed and somehow built something stronger than just performance; we had built trust. As my time in that country was coming to an end, I wanted to leave them with something that reflected what we had shared.

What do you give a team that has already given you so much?

At first, I tried to write them a single letter – a message of thanks and encouragement. It felt too impersonal, too generic.

Then I thought of writing individual notes to each person, but that, too, felt flat. None of it seemed to capture what I truly wanted to say.

One morning, while working out at home, I found myself thinking about one of them – their personality, their journey, the moments we had shared. Out of nowhere, a line of verse came to me. Just a few words, but they carried the essence of that person.

I stopped mid-set, grabbed a notebook and started writing poetry.

That first poem led to another, and then another.

Over the next few days, I wrote a short poem for each member of the team. Each one personal, heartfelt and real. Some were funny, others serious. A few revealed things I'd never said out loud before – the kind of appreciation or respect that often remains unspoken in leadership.

Then came the framing. I spent an entire day sitting on the floor surrounded by papers, frames and scraps of notes, trying to make each one feel right. Even one of my kids joined in, helping me choose the combinations that matched the mood of each person.

One question remained: How to give them away? A simple handover didn't feel right.

At our final dinner together, I told them I had prepared something special. One by one, I read each poem aloud and the team would guess who it was about.

What happened next was magic. The room filled with laughter, teasing and warmth. There were moments of silence too – the kind that carry both gratitude and grief.

When the last poem was read, nobody spoke for a moment. We just sat there, together.

It was the perfect ending – not polished or planned but deeply human. In that moment, I realised that leadership isn't only about what you build but also how you let go.

Sometimes, care is not about holding on, it's about releasing – with love, with gratitude and with grace.

Summary

Take a final moment of reflection on what you have learnt from this conclusion.

Reflection questions

- What traces am I leaving through my leadership today? Will they stand the test of time?
- Which form of care do I most often neglect when pressure rises?
- How can I make care not just an intention but a structural part of how my team operates?
- Who has cared for me along the way? How can I pay that forward?

Ask from the author

If there is one message I hope stays with you, it is this. Care is not a trend. It's not a new leadership model. It is a timeless human principle – one that becomes radical only because we forget it.

The leaders who will shape the next decade will be those who combine clarity with compassion, results with responsibility and vision with humanity. They will understand that care is not a distraction from performance – it is the condition for it.

If we, as leaders, can make care contagious – in our teams, our organisations and our communities – then maybe, just maybe, we can make leadership worthy of the trust the world has placed in us.

The Care Compass

I didn't write *The Care Factor* because I had all the answers but because I reached a point where what I knew about leadership no longer matched what I felt in it.

Early in my career, there was someone I looked up to – a loud, confident voice who seemed to have it all figured out. He spoke with authority, shared his advice generously and carried the kind of certainty that was magnetic to those of us still finding our way. A decade later, when our paths crossed again, he was still telling the same stories and jokes and giving the same advice, but this time it sounded strangely hollow. The confidence was still there, but the life had drained out of it.

That meeting stayed with me. I realised, quietly and uncomfortably, that I didn't want to become like that. For a while all I knew was what I didn't want to be. It took time to understand that real change doesn't happen through avoidance, it begins when you start defining who you aspire to be, not who you refuse to become.

When I stopped reacting against someone else's version of leadership and started shaping my own, everything began to move. The path wasn't sudden or simple. It wasn't a single decision or a grand transformation. It was a journey of learning that care isn't soft; it's slow, steady, sometimes uncertain, always human. It's choosing clarity when fear pushes you to control. It's choosing connection when urgency tempts you to withdraw. It's choosing to stay whole when the world pulls you apart.

That realisation became the seed for *The Care Factor*, and this compass grew from it. It isn't a model I invented; it's the map I needed.

Now, that same question is waiting for you: Where does your care want to go next? That's where your book begins.

Threshold: Where your book begins

The book I have written ends here, but *The Care Factor* was never meant to close. It was meant to open – into your leadership, your choices, your care.

Take a moment and find stillness, a pen and perhaps a notebook. This is not another chapter to read; it's an hour to inhabit, a quiet space to indulge in between insight and action.

The Care Compass is not a test, it's a mirror. It is an invitation to locate yourself in the landscape of care before you move forward to put my words into practice. You're not here to plan but to pause.

Ask yourself:

- Which line or story from this book has stayed with me? Why?
- Where in my leadership do I feel most alive right now?
- Where am I holding back care? What might that be protecting me from?

Science insight: The science of pause

Neuroscientists call this a meta-cognitive shift: when you think about your thinking. This activates the brain's default mode network – the system that connects memory, empathy and insight. Pausing isn't losing time, it's how awareness becomes intelligence.

The mirror: Seeing your care in four dimensions

Every leader carries an inner compass – a quiet sense of direction made of values, emotion and intent. This Care Compass helps you listen to it. It's not a measure of who you are but a mirror of how your care moves through your leadership.

Each of the four quadrants represents a dimension of care that keeps you whole and balanced. Move slowly, reflect and write. There is no score – only awareness.

1. Care for results: The discipline of clarity

Moment of truth: 'Care without clarity is kindness that confuses. Clarity without care is control that constrains.'

Care for results is the ability to hold high standards without losing humanity. It's where accountability meets compassion – where you help people to grow, not just to perform.

Ask yourself:

- When have I been most proud of a result? What kind of care made it possible?
- Where does my drive for results drift into control or fear?

- Do my expectations bring out the best in others or make them afraid to fail?
- How do I handle mine or others' mistakes?

Science insight: Goal clarity and motivation

According to Self-Determination Theory,[157] clarity fuels motivation only when it supports autonomy and purpose. External control triggers compliance; meaningful clarity inspires commitment.

Leadership lens

Clarity and care are the twin forces of sustainable performance. Without one, the other breaks.

2. Care for people: The practice of connection

Moment of truth: 'Connection begins when presence replaces performance.'

Care for people is the art of making others feel safe enough to contribute, challenge and grow. It's not about being liked; it's about being trusted.

Ask yourself:

- Whose voice have I not heard lately? Why?

- When did I last truly listen, not to reply but to understand?
- What part of me do I withhold when I feel unsafe with others?
- What does safety look like in my team? How do I shape or erode it?

Science insight: The social brain

The brain treats social rejection like physical pain.[158] When leaders create psychological safety, they calm the amygdala and re-engage the prefrontal cortex – the seat of reasoning and creativity. Safety literally unlocks intelligence.

Leadership lens

Connection doesn't slow performance, it's the precondition for it.

3. Care for self: The courage to stay whole

Moment of truth: 'You cannot pour from a cup you refuse to refill.'

Care for self is not indulgence; it's discipline. It's how you stay grounded enough to sustain others.

Ask yourself:

- What restores me – not just distracts me?
- Where do I need stronger boundaries to protect my energy and integrity?
- What signals tell me I'm running on empty? How do I respond?

Science insight: Energy and renewal

Resilience research (Fredrickson's 'broaden-and-build' theory – see Chapter 10) shows that positive emotion expands cognitive capacity and builds long-term resources. Recovery activates the parasympathetic nervous system, improving judgement and empathy.

Leadership lens

Self-care isn't selfish; it's what makes sustained care possible.

4. Care for values and community: The compass of integrity

Moment of truth: 'Integrity is what you keep doing when no one is watching.'

This is the moral north of leadership – the alignment between what you say, do and believe. It's how you expand care beyond yourself or your team.

Ask yourself:

- Which values guide my daily decisions? Which am I neglecting?
- When did I last speak up for something that mattered, even when unpopular?
- How does my work contribute to something larger than my own goals?

Science insight: Purpose and neurochemistry

Acting in line with purpose activates the brain's ventral striatum – the same reward pathway linked to motivation. Serving something bigger is literally energising.

Leadership lens

Purpose transforms effort into meaning. Meaning sustains care.

Integration: Reading your own map

You've explored the four directions of care. Now step back and look at your words, emotions and patterns. You've just drawn a map of your leadership.

Ask yourself:

- Where is my care most alive right now?
- Where is it asking for renewal or balance?
- What might imbalance be trying to teach me?

Science insight: The mechanics of change

Kurt Lewin's model shows every transformation begins with unfreeze – change – refreeze.[159] Awareness is the unfreeze. Repetition and emotion form new patterns. The brain learns through loops: cue → behaviour → emotion. By linking care to emotion, you make change stick.

Leadership lens

Awareness doesn't judge; it chooses. Every insight is a decision point.

Your first page: Designing your practice

Now move from reflection to authorship. Every story of care begins with one small, deliberate act.

On a new page, write: 'In the next 60 days, I will practise care by…'.

Finish with one specific behaviour. Then ground it in identity: 'I am the kind of leader who…'.

Protect yourself by choosing something small but sacred:

- Protect one hour of deep work each week.
- Ask one person, 'How are you – really?'
- Say no once where you used to say yes.

Science insight: How habits grow

Big change starts small. Start tiny and make it easy to win.[160] Anchor it to a daily cue.

Celebrate, as emotion not repetition wires the habit.

Reflect, as attention strengthens neuroplasticity.

Leadership lens

Change is less about force than fluency – aligning daily behaviour with who you wish to be.

Passing the pen

This is where *The Care Factor* ends and its purpose begins. From this point, you are the author. Every act of clarity, connection, courage and integrity adds another line to a story that only you can write.

This story won't be printed. It will be lived – through choices, presence and care.

Moment of truth: Leadership is not what you know; it's how you show up when it matters.

Take your compass, pick up your pen and begin.

Notes

1 C Lindgren (ed.), *Bondepraktikan* (1508)
2 CAE Goodhart, *Problems of Monetary Management: The UK experience* (Reserve Bank of Australia, 1975)
3 D Harper, 'Decide', *Online Etymology Dictionary* (2001), www.etymonline.com/search?q=decide, accessed 22 January 2026
4 H Schultz and J Gordon, *Onward: How Starbucks fought for its life without losing its soul* (Rodale, 2011)
5 D Hounshell and JK Smith, *Science and Corporate Strategy: Du Pont R&D, 1902–1980* (Cambridge University Press, 1988)
6 JK Liker, *The Toyota Way: 14 management principles from the world's greatest manufacturer* (McGraw-Hill, 2004)
7 HB Perry, et al., *Community Health Workers and Health Systems* (World Health Organization, 2017)
8 J Collins, *Good to Great: Why some companies make the leap… and others don't* (HarperBusiness, 2001)
9 JM Kouzes and BZ Posner, *The Leadership Challenge: How to make extraordinary things happen in organizations* (Wiley, 2017)
10 PF Drucker, *The Practice of Management* (Harper & Row, 1954)
11 WE Deming, *Out of the Crisis* (MIT Press, 1986)

12 TM Amabile and SJ Kramer, *The Progress Principle: Using small wins to ignite joy, engagement, and creativity at work* (Harvard Business Review Press, 2011)

13 N Mandela, *Long Walk to Freedom: The autobiography of Nelson Mandela* (Little, Brown and Company, 1994)

14 World Health Organization, *WHO Surgical Safety Checklist* (2009), www.who.int/docs/default-source/patient-safety/9789241598590-eng-checklist.pdf, accessed 22 January 2026

15 International Monetary Fund, *Global Financial Stability Report: Financial stress and deleveraging* (October 2008), www.imf.org/-/media/websites/imf/imported-full-text-pdf/external/pubs/ft/gfsr/2008/02/pdf/_text.pdf, accessed 22 January 2026

16 MC Jensen, 'Value Maximization, Stakeholder Theory, and the Corporate Objective Function', *Journal of Applied Corporate Finance*, 7/3 (2001), 219–317, www.efmaefm.org/bharat/jensen_efm2001.pdf, accessed 22 January 2026

17 J Ewing, *Faster, Higher, Farther: The Volkswagen scandal* (W. W. Norton & Company, 2017)

18 P Wiessner, 'Embers of Society: Firelight talk among the Ju/'hoansi Bushmen', *Proceedings of the National Academy of Sciences* (7 August 2014), https://doi.org/10.1073/pnas.1404212111

19 K Eschner, updated by S Anderson, 'What Happened to the Canary in the Coal Mine? The Story of How the Real-Life Animal Helper Became Just a Metaphor', *Smithsonian Magazine* (7 March 2024), www.smithsonianmag.com/smart-news/what-happened-canary-coal-mine-story-how-real-life-animal-helper-became-just-metaphor-180961570, accessed 12 February 2026

20 A Edmondson, *The Fearless Organization: Creating psychological safety in the workplace for learning, innovation and growth* (Wiley, 2018)

21 DA Garvin, AB Wagonfeld and L Kind, *Google's Project Oxygen: Do managers matter?* (Harvard Business School Case, 2013)

22 S Nadella, *Hit Refresh: The quest to rediscover Microsoft's soul and imagine a better future for everyone* (Harper Business, 2017)

23 WF Whyte and KK Whyte, *Making Mondragon: The growth and dynamics of the worker cooperative complex* (ILR Press, 1991)

24 M Isaac, *Super Pumped: The battle for Uber* (W. W. Norton & Company, 2017)

25 D Rock, 'SCARF: A brain-based model for collaborating with and influencing others', *NeuroLeadership Journal*, 1 (2008), https://schoolguide.casel.org/uploads/sites/2/2018/12/SCARF-NeuroleadershipArticle.pdf, accessed 26 January 2026

26 D Goleman, *Emotional Intelligence* (Bantam Books, 1995)

27 Aristotle, *Nicomachean Ethics* (Penguin Classic, 2020)

28 MP Follett, *Creative Experience* (Longmans, Green and Company, 1924)

29 Gallup, *State of the Global Workplace* (2025), www.gallup.com/workplace/349484/state-of-the-global-workplace.aspx, accessed 26 January 2026

30 R Service, *Stalin: A Biography* (Harvard University Press, 2004)

31 J Herway, 'Is Quiet Quitting Real?, Gallup (6 September 2022, updated 17 May 2023), www.gallup.com/workplace/398306/quiet-quitting-real.aspx, accessed 12 February 2026

32 United Nations Environment Programme, *The Importance of Mangroves to People: A call to action* (2014), www.unep.org/resources/report/importance-mangroves-people-call-action, accessed 26 January 2026

33 International Civil Aviation Organization, *Cabin Safety Procedures and Passenger Briefings*, ICAO Guidelines

34 IOC Medical and Scientific Commission, 'The International Olympic Committee (IOC) Consensus Statement on Periodic Health Evaluation of Elite Athletes: March 2009', *Journal of Athletic Training*, 44/5 (Sep–Oct 2009), 538–557, http://doi.org/10.4085/1062-6050-44.5.538

35 C-M Tan, *Search Inside Yourself: The unexpected path to achieving success, happiness (and world peace)* (HarperOne, 2012)

36 Microsoft Japan, *Work-Life Choice Challenge 2019 Summer* (Microsoft Corporation, 2019)

37 Y Chouinard, *Let My People Go Surfing: The education of a reluctant businessman* (Penguin, 2006)

38 Médecins Sans Frontières, *Staff Health, Well-being and Psychological Support Policies* (MSF Operational Centre, n.d.)

39 J Weststar, V O'Meara and M-J Legault, *Developer Satisfaction Survey 2017: Summary report*, International Game Developers Association (8 January 2018), https://igda-website.s3.us-east-2.amazonaws.com/wp-content/uploads/2019/04/11143720/IGDA_DSS_2017_SummaryReport.pdf, accessed 27 January 2026

40 D Harris, *10% Happier: How I tamed the voice in my head, reduced stress without losing my edge, and found the self-help that actually works* (HarperCollins, 2014)
41 G Massie, '"I've got nothing left in the tank": Jacinda Ardern's resignation speech in full', *Independent* (19 January 2023), www.independent.co.uk/world/jacinda-ardern-resignation-prime-minister-new-zealand-speech-b2265319.html, accessed 12 February 2026
42 A Huffington, *The Sleep Revolution: Transforming your life, one night at a time* (Harmony Books, 2016)
43 J Clear, *Atomic Habits: An easy and proven way to build good habits and break bad ones* (Avery, 2018)
44 D Buettner, *The Blue Zones: 9 lessons for living longer from the people who've lived the longest* (National Geographic Books, 2012)
45 D Nikel, 'Swedish Fika: Sweden's "Premium Coffee Break" Explained', *Forbes* (3 January 2023), www.forbes.com/sites/davidnikel/2023/01/03/swedish-fika-swedens-premium-coffee-break-explained, accessed 12 February 2026
46 BJ Park, et al., 'The Physiological Effects of *Shinrin-yoku* (Taking in the Forest Atmosphere of Forest Bathing): Evidence from field experiments in 24 forests across Japan', *Environmental Health and Preventive Medicine*, 15/1 (2 May 2009), 18–26, https://doi.org/10.1007/s12199-009-0086-9
47 J Needham, *Science and Civilisation in China: Volume 4, physics and physical technology* (Cambridge University Press, 1986)
48 Oxford English Dictionary, *Whistleblower*, www.oed.com/dictionary/whistle-blower, accessed 27 January 2026
49 D Ellsberg, *Secrets: A memoir of Vietnam and the Pentagon Papers* (Viking, 2002)
50 Whistleblower Network News, 'Opinion: The memo that brought down Enron' (28 November 2019), https://whistleblowersblog.org/opinion/the-memo-that-brought-down-enron, accessed 12 February 2026
51 Congress.gov, 'S.Hrg. 117-769 — PROTECTING KIDS ONLINE: TESTIMONY FROM A FACEBOOK WHISTLEBLOWER', Senate Hearing (5 November 2021), www.congress.gov/event/117th-congress/senate-event/330603/text, accessed 12 February 2026
52 B McLean and P Elkind, *The Smartest Guys in the Room: The amazing rise and scandalous fall of Enron* (Portfolio, 2003)

53 Consumer Financial Protection Bureau, 'Consumer Financial Protection Bureau Fines Wells Fargo $100 Million for Widespread Illegal Practice of Secretly Opening Unauthorized Accounts' (8 September 2016), www.consumerfinance.gov/about-us/newsroom/consumer-financial-protection-bureau-fines-wells-fargo-100-million-widespread-illegal-practice-secretly-opening-unauthorized-accounts, accessed 12 February 2026

54 United States National Transportation Safety Board, *Marine Accident Report: Grounding of the U.S. tankship, Exxon Valdez On Bligh Reef, Prince William Sound near Valdez, Alaska, March 24, 1989* (The Board, 1990)

55 J Carreyrou, *Bad Blood: Secrets and lies in a Silicon Valley startup* (Knopf, 2018)

56 D Gelles, N Kitroeff, J Nicas and R Ruiz, 'Boeing Was "Go, Go, Go" to Beat Airbus With the 737 Max', *The New York Times* (23 March 2019), www.nytimes.com/2019/03/23/business/boeing-737-max-crash.html, accessed 12 February 2026

57 B Snyder, 'Unilever CEO: Refocus Your Ambitions,' Insights by Stanford Business (21 June 2016), www.gsb.stanford.edu/insights/unilever-ceo-refocus-your-ambitions, accessed 12 March 2026

58 M Evers, 'New Campaign Asks Customers to be #TravelKind', Transport for London (13 November 2017), https://tfl.gov.uk/info-for/media/press-releases/2017/november/new-campaign-asks-customers-to-be-travelki, accessed 27 January 2026

59 R Spector, *The Nordstrom Way to Customer Service Excellence: A handbook for implementing great service in your organization* (Wiley, 2005)

60 IL Janis, *Victims of Groupthink: A psychological study of foreign policy decisions and fiascos* (Houghton Mifflin, 1972)

61 D Vaughan, *The Challenger Launch Decision* (University of Chicago Press, 1996)

62 C Boddy, *Corporate Psychopaths: Organizational destroyers* (Palgrave Macmillan, 2011)

63 D Harper, 'Innovation', *Online Etymology Dictionary*, www.etymonline.com/search?q=innovation, accessed 27 January 2026

64 R Barrangou, et al., 'CRISPR Provides Acquired Resistance Against Viruses in Prokaryotes,' *Science*, 315/5819 (23 March 2007), 1709–12, http://doi.org/10.1126/science.1138140

65 Médecins Sans Frontières, *Access to Medicines*, https://msf.org.uk/issues/access-medicines, accessed 27 January 2026
66 M Yunus, *Banker to the Poor: Micro-lending and the battle against world poverty* (PublicAffairs, 2007)
67 National Academy of Sciences, *Funding a Revolution: Government support for computing research* (1999), https://doi.org/10.17226/6323
68 Team Pepper, 'Marketing Case Study: The Story Behind Tata Nano's Failure as a Brand', Pepper (5 May 2022), www.pepper.inc/blog/why-tata-nano-branding-was-a-failure, accessed 12 February 2026
69 Bill & Melinda Gates Foundation, *Global Grand Challenges*, https://gcgh.grandchallenges.org, accessed 27 January 2026
70 CM Christensen, *The Innovator's Dilemma: When new technologies cause great firms to fall* (Harvard Business School Press, 1997)
71 PF Drucker, *Innovation and Entrepreneurship: Practice and principles* (Harper & Row, 1985)
72 M Mazzucato, *The Entrepreneurial State: Debunking public vs. private sector myths* (Anthem Press, 2013)
73 T Brown, *Change by Design: How design thinking transforms organizations and inspires innovation* (Harper Business, 2009)
74 Transport for London, *Priority Seating and Other Features On Board*, https://tfl.gov.uk/transport-accessibility/features-on-board, accessed 27 January 2026
75 TC Bestor, *Tsukiji: The fish market at the center of the world* (University of California Press, 2004)
76 D Hounshell and JK Smith, *Science and Corporate Strategy: Du Pont R&D, 1902–1980* (Cambridge University Press, 1988)
77 M Lynch, 'The Demise Of The Segway Is A Cautionary Tale For Technological Optimists', *Forbes* (29 June 2020), www.forbes.com/sites/michaellynch/2020/06/29/the-demise-of-the-segway-is-a-cautionary-tale-for-technological-optimists, accessed 12 February 2026
78 HC Lucas and JM Goh, 'Disruptive Technology: How Kodak missed the digital photography revolution', *Journal of Strategic Information Systems*, 18/1 (March 2009), 46–55, https://doi.org/10.1016/j.jsis.2009.01.002
79 G Satell, 'A Look Back At Why Blockbuster Really Failed And Why It Didn't Have To', *Forbes* (5 September 2014,

updated 10 December 2021), www.forbes.com/sites/gregsatell/2014/09/05/a-look-back-at-why-blockbuster-really-failed-and-why-it-didnt-have-to, accessed 12 February 2026

80 Food and Agriculture Organization of the United Nations, *FAOSTAT: Crops and livestock products* (2025), www.fao.org/faostat/en/#data/QCL, accessed 28 January 2026

81 CJ Nemeth, *In Defense of Troublemakers: The Power of dissent in life and business* (Basic Books, 2018)

82 DA Thomas and RJ Ely, 'Making Differences Matter: A new paradigm for managing diversity', *Harvard Business Review* (September–October 1996), https://hbr.org/1996/09/making-differences-matter-a-new-paradigm-for-managing-diversity, accessed 28 January 2026

83 Cloverpop, *Hacking Diversity with Inclusive Decision Making* (2017), https://cloverpop.com/hubfs/Whitepapers/Cloverpop_Hacking_Diversity_Inclusive_Decision_Making_White_Paper.pdf, accessed 28 January 2026

84 LEGO Group, *Celebrating 60 Years of LEGO® Bricks and Endless Creativity*, 25 January 2018, https://lego.com/en-us/aboutus/news/2019/october/lego-60th-anniversary, accessed 28 January 2026

85 IBM, *Diversity, Equity and Inclusion*, https://ibm.com/history/diversity-policies, accessed 28 January 2026

86 Unilever, *Equality, Diversity and Inclusion*, https://unilever.com/sustainability/equity-diversity-and-inclusion, accessed 28 January 2026

87 S Fowler, *Whistle Blower: My journey to Silicon Valley and fight for justice at Uber* (Penguin Random House, 2021)

88 Médecins Sans Frontières, *Upholding Diversity, Equality, and Inclusion at MSF*, https://doctorswithoutborders.org/who-we-are/commitment-to-DEI, accessed 28 January 2026

89 YM Antorini, AM Muñiz and T Askildsen, 'Collaborating with Customer Communities: Lessons from the Lego Group', *MIT Sloan Management Review* (20 March 2012), https://sloanreview.mit.edu/article/collaborating-with-customer-communities-lessons-from-the-lego-group, accessed 28 January 2026

90 S Page, *The Difference – How the Power of Diversity Creates Better Groups, Firms, Schools and Societies* (Princeton University Press, 2007)

91 H Bresman and AC Edmondson, 'Research: To Excel, Diverse Teams Need Psychological Safety', *Harvard*

Business Review (17 March 2022), https://hbr.org/2022/03/research-to-excel-diverse-teams-need-psychological-safety, accessed 12 February 2026

92 RM Kanter and RJ Ely, 'Celebrating "The Men and Women of the Corporation" 40 Years Later', Harvard Business School (10 September 2018), www.library.hbs.edu/working-knowledge/celebrating-the-men-and-women-of-the-corporation-40-years-later, accessed 12 February 2026

93 F Johansson, *The Medici Effect: Breakthrough insights at the intersection of ideas, concepts and cultures* (Harvard Business Review Press, 2004)

94 M Wiking, *The Little Book of Hygge: The Danish way to live well* (Penguin Life, 2016)

95 UNESCO Intangible Cultural Heritage, *Hawker Culture in Singapore: Community, dining and culinary practices in a multicultural urban context*, https://ich.unesco.org/en/RL/hawker-culture-in-singapore-community-dining-and-culinary-practices-in-a-multicultural-urban-context-01568, accessed 28 January 2026

96 JB Strauss, *The Building of the Golden Gate Bridge* (McGraw-Hill, 1938)

97 S Sinek, 'A community is a group of people who agree to grow together', Facebook (17 July 2018), www.facebook.com/simonsinek/posts/a-community-is-a-group-of-people-who-agree-to-grow-together/10156532240696499/#, accessed 12 February 2026

98 D Harper, 'Community', *Online Etymology Dictionary*, https://etymonline.com/search?q=community, accessed 28 January 2026

99 Y Chouinard, *Let My People Go Surfing: The education of a reluctant businessman* (Penguin, 2006)

100 R Levering and M Moskowitz, *The 100 Best Companies to Work For* (Fortune, 2016)

101 Habitat for Humanity, *Impact*, https://habitat.org/our-work/impact, accessed 28 January 2026

102 B Roy, *Women Barefeet Solar Engineers: A community solution*, United Nations Commission on the Status of Women (22 February–4 March 2011), https://un.org/womenwatch/daw/csw/csw55/panels/Panel1-Roy-Bunker.pdf, accessed 28 January 2026

103 J Kantor and D Streitfeld, 'Inside WeWork's Culture of Excess and Control', *The New York Times* (2019)

104 E Pariser, *The Filter Bubble: What the internet is hiding from you* (Penguin Press, 2011)
105 Stanford Encyclopedia of Philosophy, 'Martin Buber' (20 April 2004, updated 28 July 2020), https://plato.stanford.edu/entries/buber, accessed 12 February 2026
106 The Nobel Prize, 'Elinor Ostrom' (n.d.), www.nobelprize.org/prizes/economic-sciences/2009/ostrom/lecture, accessed 12 February 2026
107 B Brown, 'The Power of Vulnerability', TedTalk (1 June 2010), https://brenebrown.com/videos/ted-talk-the-power-of-vulnerability, accessed 12 February 2026
108 E and B Wenger-Trayner, 'Introduction to communities of practice', Wenger-Trayner (June 2015), www.wenger-trayner.com/introduction-to-communities-of-practice, accessed 12 February 2026
109 B Gustavsson, *Bildningens väg* (Daidalos, 1991)
110 ES Raymond, *The Cathedral and the Bazaar* (O'Reilly Media, 1999)
111 RD Putnam, *Bowling Alone: The collapse and revival of American community* (Simon & Schuster, 2000)
112 J Holt-Lunstad, TB Smith and JB Layton, 'Social Relationships and Mortality Risk: A meta-analytic review', *PLoS Medicine*, 7/7 (July 2010), http://doi.org/10.1371/journal.pmed.1000316
113 A Davidson, *Hot Sauce Nation: America's burning obsession* (Little, Brown and Company, 2015)
114 H Ebbinghaus, *Über das Gedächtnis: Untersuchungen zur experimentellen psychologie* (Duncker & Humblot, 1885)
115 J Kerr, *Legacy* (Constable, 2013)
116 M Singer, 'Inside SodaStream's Turnaround', *The New York Times* (2018)
117 J Kantor and D Streitfeld, 'Inside WeWork's Culture of Excess and Control,' *The New York Times* (2019)
118 B Watson, *The Analects of Confucius* (Columbia University Press, 2009)
119 CS Dweck, *Mindset: The new psychology of success* (Random House, 2006)
120 PM Senge, *The Fifth Discipline* (Doubleday, 1990)
121 C Argyris and D Schön, *Organizational Learning: A theory of action perspective* (Addison-Wesley, 1978)
122 J Mezirow, *Transformative Dimensions of Adult Learning* (Jossey-Bass, 1991)

123 University of the Third Age, *About us*, https://u3a.org.uk/about, accessed 28 January 2026
124 DC Park and P Reuter-Lorenz, 'The Adaptive Brain: Aging and neurocognitive scaffolding', *Psychological Review*, 60 (January 2009), 173–96, http://doi.org/10.1146/annurev.psych.59.103006.093656
125 E Wenger, *Communities of Practice: Learning, Meaning, and Identity* (Cambridge University Press, 1998)
126 B Mediratta, 'The Google Way: Give engineers room', *The New York Times* (21 October 2007), https://nytimes.com/2007/10/21/jobs/21pre.html, accessed 29 January 2026
127 LinkedIn, *LinkedIn Learning: Develop skills that move your career forward*, www.linkedin.com/learning, accessed 29 January 2026
128 J Sweller, 'Cognitive Load During Problem Solving: Effects on learning', *Cognitive Science* (April 1988), https://doi.org/10.1207/s15516709cog1202_4
129 B Hedberg, 'How Organizations Learn and Unlearn' in *Organization Studies* (Oxford University Press, 1981)
130 Wikipedia, Gary Anderson (Designer), https://en.wikipedia.org/wiki/Gary_Anderson_(designer), accessed 29 January 2026
131 World Commission on Environment and Development, *Our Common Future* (Oxford University Press, 1987)
132 P Baldrian, 'Forest Microbiome: Diversity, complexity and dynamics', *FEMS Microbiology Reviews*, 41/2 (March 2017), 109–130, https://doi.org/10.1093/femsre/fuw040
133 Patagonia, 'Don't Buy This Jacket, Black Friday and the New York Times' (25 November 2011), www.patagonia.com/stories/planet/activism/dont-buy-this-jacket-black-friday-and-the-new-york-times/story-18615.html, accessed 12 February 2026
134 IKEA, *Transitioning Towards a Circular Business*, https://ikea.com/global/en/our-business/sustainability/our-circular-agenda, accessed 29 January 2026
135 Unilever, *A New Era of Corporate Sustainability*, https://unilever.com/sustainability, accessed 29 January 2026
136 World Health Organization, *Blood Safety and Availability*, https://who.int/news-room/fact-sheets/detail/blood-safety-and-availability, accessed 29 January 2026
137 DH Meadows, DL Meadows, J Randers and W Behrens, *The Limits to Growth* (Universe Books, 1972)

138 J Elkington, *Cannibals with Forks: The triple bottom line of 21st century business* (Capstone, 1997)
139 K Raworth, *Doughnut Economics: 7 ways to think like a 21st century economist* (Chelsea Green Publishing, 2017)
140 RW Kimmerer, *Braiding Sweetgrass: Indigenous wisdom, scientific knowledge and the teaching of plants* (Milkweed Editions, 2013)
141 M Solomon, 'Heroic Customer Service: When Ritz-Carlton Saved Thomas The Tank Engine', *Forbes* (15 January 2015), www.forbes.com/sites/micahsolomon/2015/01/15/the-amazing-true-story-of-the-hotel-that-saved-thomas-the-tank-engine, accessed 26 February 2026
142 JR Jambeck, 'Plastic Waste Inputs from Land into the Ocean', *Science*, 347/6223 (13 February 2015), 768–771, http://doi.org/10.1126/science.1260352
143 HA Leslie, et al., 'Discovery and Quantification of Plastic Particles in Human Blood', *Environment International*, 163 (May 2022), https://doi.org/10.1016/j.envint.2022.107199
144 MA Delmas and VC Burbano, 'The Drivers of Greenwashing', *California Management Review*, 54/1 (1 October 2011), https://doi.org/10.1525/cmr.2011.54.1.64
145 F Berg, JF Kölbel and R Rigobon, 'Aggregate Confusion: The divergence of ESG ratings', *Review of Finance*, 26/6 (23 May 2022), 1315–1344, https://doi.org/10.1093/rof/rfac033
146 Welsh Government, *The Well-being of Future Generations*, https://gov.wales/well-being-of-future-generations-wales, accessed 29 January 2026
147 B Latané and JM Darley, *The Unresponsive Bystander: Why doesn't he help?* (Appleton-Century-Crofts, 1970)
148 BL Fredrickson, *Positivity: Groundbreaking research reveals how to embrace the hidden strength of positive emotions, overcome negativity, and thrive* (Crown Publishing Group, 2009)
149 MT Roth, *Law Collections from Mesopotamia and Asia Minor* (Scholars Press, 1997), https://doi.org/10.2307/jj.25577265
150 V Havel, 'Politics and Conscience' in *Living in Truth* (Faber & Faber, 1986)
151 BL Fredrickson, 'The Role of Positive Emotions in Positive Psychology: The broaden-and-build theory of positive emotions,' *American Psychologist*, 56/3 (2001), 218–226, https://doi.org/10.1037/0003-066X.56.3.218
152 D Tutu, *God Has a Dream: A vision of hope for our time* (Image Books, 2011)

153 United Nations, *A New Era of Conflict and Violence*, https://un.org/en/un75/new-era-conflict-and-violence, accessed 29 January 2026

154 Intergovernmental Panel on Climate Change, *AR6 Synthesis Report: Climate Change 2023* (2023), www.ipcc.ch/report/ar6/syr, accessed 29 January 2026

155 RD Putnam, *Bowling Alone: The collapse and revival of American community* (Simon & Schuster, 2000)

156 MEP Seligman, *Flourish: A visionary new understanding of happiness and well-being* (Free Press, 2011)

157 RM Ryan and EL Deci, 'Intrinsic and Extrinsic Motivation from a Self-Determination Theory Perspective: Definitions, theory, practices, and future definitions', *Contemporary Educational Psychology*, 61 (2020), https://doi.org/10.1016/j.cedpsych.2020.101860

158 NI Eisenberger and MD Lieberman, 'Why Rejection Hurts: A common neural alarm system for physical and social pain', *Trends in Cognitive Sciences*, 8/7 (2004), 294–300, https://doi.org/10.1016/j.tics.2004.05.010

159 M Raza, 'Lewin's 3 Stage Model of Change Explained', *BMC* (December 20, 2024), www.bmc.com/blogs/lewin-three-stage-model-change, accessed 29 January 2026

160 BJ Fogg, *Tiny Habits: The small changes that change everything* (Virgin Digital, 2019)

Acknowledgements

Writing *The Care Factor* has been both a journey of reflection and a practice of care in itself. Along the way, I've been reminded that leadership – like writing – is rarely a solo act. Every idea in these pages has roots in the people who have challenged, encouraged and cared for me over many years.

First and foremost, to Elisabeth, who always supports my crazy ideas – often long before I've figured out what they actually are. Thank you for your patience, your steady belief and for creating the calm, beautiful balance that made this work possible.

To the early readers who engaged so generously with the manuscript – your insights, honesty and encouragement gave shape and depth to the message. You know who you are, and I am eternally grateful.

To the many leaders, teams and colleagues I've had the privilege to work with over the years – thank you for showing me what care in leadership looks like when lived, not just spoken about. You've inspired many of the stories, questions and paradoxes that fill these pages.

To those who, at times, believed in me even more than I dared to believe in myself – thank you. Your confidence has been both a mirror and a compass.

Finally, to everyone who chooses to lead with care in a world that often forgets its importance – this book is for you. May it offer something of value in return for all the care I've been fortunate to receive.

The Author

Håkan Johansson has spent more than three decades leading people and organisations across the world – from California to London, from Stockholm to the sunlit hills of northern Italy. As a senior executive in global healthcare, he has guided teams through transformation, growth and uncertainty, learning that what sustains performance is not pressure but care.

Today, as Head of Europe, South-East at Roche Diagnostics, Håkan continues to work at the intersection of business and humanity, where results are driven not by command but by connection.

The Care Factor is born from those years of experience: a reflection on what truly makes leadership work when the stakes are high and the pace is fast. It is both a philosophy and a practice – grounded in courage, clarity and genuine human care.

Håkan lives in Switzerland. Together with his wife, he also runs a small farm in southern Sweden – a place where ideas, vines and values are cultivated side by side.

🌐 www.thecarefactor.ch

www.ingramcontent.com/pod-product-compliance
Lightning Source LLC
LaVergne TN
LVHW030917080826
845145LV00013B/2942

* 9 7 8 1 7 8 1 3 3 9 8 2 4 *